The Deepening Complexity of

CROP CIRCLES

Beckhampton, England, 1998.

Photograph © Dr. Andrew King.

The Deepening Complexity of

Broadbury Banks, England, 2000.
Photograph © Bert Janssen.

CROP CIRCLES

Scientific
Research
& Urban
Legends

Eltjo H. Haselhoff, Ph.D.

Frog Books
Berkeley, California

Published by Frog Books

Frog Books' publications are distributed by
North Atlantic Books
P.O. Box 12327
Berkeley, California 94712

Cover photograph: Woodborough Hill, England, 2000, © Bert Janssen.
Cover and book design by Paula Morrison

Printed in the United States of America

The Deepening Compexity of Crop Circles is sponsored by the Society for the Study of Native Arts and Sciences, a nonprofit educational corporation whose goals are to develop an educational and cross-cultural perspective linking various scientific, social, and artistic fields; to nurture a holistic view of arts, sciences, humanities, and healing; and to publish and distribute literature on the relationship of mind, body, and nature.

North Atlantic Books' publications are available through most bookstores. For further information, visit our Web site at www.northatlanticbooks.com or call 800-733-3000.

ISBN-13: 978-1-58394-046-4

Library of Congress Cataloging-in-Publication Data

Haselhoff, Eltjo, 1962–
    The deepening complexity of crop circles : scientific research and urban legends / by Eltjo Haselhoff.
        p. cm.
        ISBN 1-58394-046-4 (alk. paper)
        1. Science—Miscellanea. 2. Crop Circles—Miscellanea. 3. Curiosities and wonders—Miscellanea. I. Title.
    Q173.H365 2001
    001.94—dc21

                                                                2001016178

4 5 6 7 8 9 UNITED 14 13 12 11 10

To my beloved family,
Michela, Alexander, Rebecca

The famous "Koch Fractal" of Milk Hill, England, 1997, one of the most intricate
formations that have ever appeared.
Photograph © Dr. Andrew King.

Acknowledgments

I COULD NEVER WRITE A BOOK ALL BY MYSELF. I WOULD LIKE TO THANK TREVOR Dawkins for textual corrections, and in particular Dr. Scott Flamm, who spent a large amount of his time carefully reading the manuscript, and who came up with numerous valuable suggestions for improvement. Scott, without your great help this book would have been different. Thank you so much! Bert Janssen and Janet Ossebaard, two leading Dutch crop circle researchers, most kindly donated a valuable collection of professional and highly artistic photographic material, which completely changed the character of this book. Bert and Janet, I owe much gratitude to both of you and I am proud to have you among my friends. Thanks also to Dr. Uwe Engelmann, Arjan Dekker, ilyes, Nancy Talbott, and Dr. William Levengood for more photographic donations. Many thanks to Dr. Andrew King and Ron Russell. Thanks to Peter Sørensen. Thanks to Robbert van den Broeke for the use of his photograph, field assistance, and for sharing his extraordinary experiences with me. Thanks to Michael Newark, Bob Snackers, Riet de Graaf, Jaap van Etten, Robert Boerman, Paola Harris, Maurizio Baiata, the famous Italian talk show host Maurizio Costanzo, and my Italian friends Caterina Rigato, Davide Cuccato, and in particular Tarcisio Fiabane. Many thanks also to my parents for their continuing enthusiasm and support, and especially to my beautiful and beloved wife, Michela, for her unconditional love and encouragement. Thanks to all crop circle researchers, crop circle lovers, crop circle skeptics, crop circle debunkers, and crop circle hoaxers, who help to make the crop circles a fascinating phenomenon of our time. And last but not least, thanks to the mysterious Circlemakers, without whom this book never would have been written.

"Those who are unqualified to judge should refrain from comment."
—George Terence Meaden, Ph.D.

Allington Down, England, 1999.
Photograph © Ron Russell.

West Kennet, England, 1999.
Photograph © Dr. Andrew King.

Contents

Uffington, England, 2000.
Photograph © Bert Janssen.

Preface

When I read a book, I usually skip the preface. Most of the time, after reading a few lines, I find it boring, too long, and not to the point. I hope this is not your habit too, because this preface contains some important notes that reflect upon the rest of this book.

ALTHOUGH THERE ARE MANY INDICATIONS THAT CROP CIRCLES HAVE appeared for a very long time, the study of the phenomenon is still relatively young. Over a few decades many interested people, all with different backgrounds, have studied crop circles from many different perspectives and produced an abundance of results. The interested reader only needs to access the Internet and look for articles related to "crop circle" to find enough reading material for a very long vacation. Because the study of crop circles, sometimes referred to as *cerealogy*, is so young, no reference standards yet exist. There is no university with a department of cerealogy, and consequently anyone may call him- or herself a "cerealogist," even after one single visit to a crop circle (or fewer). Without intending to criticize anyone in particular, it is my opinion that many of the conclusions that have been reached over the years by self-proclaimed crop circle researchers were premature. Many speculative arguments have been presented without solid and objective evidence. This was not only done by crop circle enthusiasts, often referred to as *believers* by the more skeptical participants in the crop circle adventure, but it certainly also holds for many—if not most—of these skeptics themselves. Innumerable heated discussions between these two groups have taken place (often this seems to be the main activity in and around the crop circles); however, most of these communications seem to be based on emotions and "gut feelings" only. On both sides conclusions always come first, after which reasons and arguments are collected in order to support these. Many times these arguments are indecisive, incomplete, or even completely wrong, despite the sometimes apparently intellectual contents.

After studying the crop circle phenomenon for thirteen years, I have learned much, but many questions still remain, while new questions have arisen. Consequently, I have come to the conclusion that the crop circle phenomenon is not so simple. During the study of crop circles, utter caution is a prerequisite, and the researcher should proceed slowly and step-by-step. First, all facts should be observed carefully, during which you have to take care to remain on the narrow and thorny path between an open mind and skepticism. Then (and only then) you can analyze the observations and try to make them match the part of the world that we have studied already and which we understand. If the observations do not fit your experiences, you should not jump to conclusions, but think twice, check and double-check. You should be aware of the limits of human knowledge, but in particular the limits of your own knowledge (the latter defines a wise man, according to the ancient Greeks). You will have to talk to others and approach specialists. Ultimately, you may try to come up with a hypothesis about what might have been the case. It is this approach that will be used throughout this book, in particular in Chapters One to Three. Only in Chapter Four will I clearly jump over the cliff of rational analysis and present viewpoints from people who approach the crop circle phenomenon with their emotions only. Chapter Five concludes.

This book will not tell you how all crop circles are made. It will not tell you where they all come from, and it only suggests what they might mean. I don't believe any other author could do more. This book will show you all the facts, however, and also all the fiction. It will teach you how to approach this fascinating phenomenon that occurs all over the world, and which is often so much underestimated in its complexity. It is an attempt to make a clean sweep of the interminable discussions by news reporters, skeptics, debunkers, crop circle fanatics, and others, which have completely covered up the essence of it all. And at the end, I trust you will be impressed.

Enjoy!

Dr. Eltjo H. Haselhoff

The Deepening Complexity of
CROP CIRCLES

Brummen, Holland, 1997.
Photograph © Eltjo Haselhoff.

Chapter 1

A Worldwide and Most Tangible Mystery

During the last decades, more and more people have been fascinated by a curious phenomenon: the appearance of complex, most accurately designed geometric patterns in fields all over the world, in which vegetation is squeezed flat against the ground. In the vernacular these geometrical formations of flattened crops were soon called "crop circles," because the first known events consisted of circular imprints only. However, the phenomenon escalated to eye-catching and complicated geometrical pictograms, manifesting themselves in all sorts of vegetation and also in ice, snow, and sand. Nevertheless, the appellation "crop circle" has settled down to such an extent that we will use the name throughout this book.

The Development of a Worldwide Enigma

CONTRARY TO GENERAL BELIEF, CROP CIRCLES ARE NOT A RECENT PHEnomenon. A famous account that was recorded on August 22, 1678, describes without much doubt the appearance of crop circles in a field of oats near Hertfordshire, England. In those days this was seen as the work of the devil, who "scorn'd to mow them after the usual manner, and cut them in round circles, and plac't every straw with that exactness that it would have taken up above an Age for any Man to perform what he did that one night." It seems, however, that the crop might have been flattened only, rather than mowed, as illustrated by the accompanying diagram. (See Figure 1-1.) It shows a little devil-like creature, who seems to lay many crop stems neatly aligned, flat against the soil. The perfect, spiraled alignment of the flattened

Figure 1-1. "The Mowing Devil," 1687.

crop, together with the very obvious circular shape, is most striking. Anyone who has ever seen a crop circle in real life will have little doubt that the artist who created the image of the "Mowing Devil" intended to represent the same thing that we see in our fields today.

One year earlier, in his work *The Natural History of Staffordshire,* the British scientist Robert Plot suggested that crop formations (including square and hexagonal patterns!) were the effect of airflows falling down from the sky. (Interestingly, this statement was independently repeated four hundred years later, after intensive studies, by one of the most profound scientific crop circle researchers, Dr. George Terence Meaden.) Many people, particularly in the south of England, have reported the appearance of crop formations since the beginning of the twentieth century. One of the early crop circle researchers, the Englishman Colin Andrews, writes about formations reported in the fifties.[1] Dr. Terence Meaden reported about one hundred circles prior to 1980.[2] In 1999, I met an old English gentleman in Avebury who said to me: "These circles have appeared in the fields ever since I was a little boy. We used to play in them, it was fun. They came back almost every year. And all of a sudden everybody is making all this fuss about it." Nevertheless, it is a fact that since the late seventies the number of crop circle appearances has increased dramatically, particularly in the south of England, in the

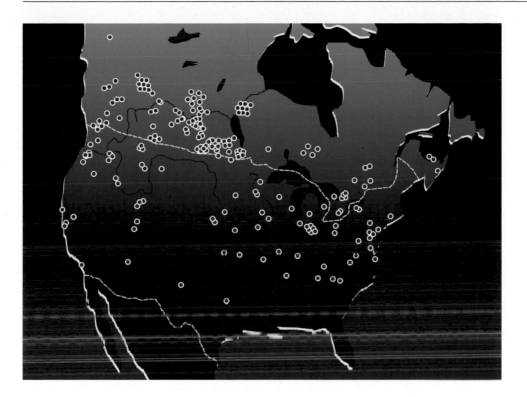

Figure 1-2. Reported crop circles in the USA and Canada, from the earliest known formation in Hubbard, Oregon (1964), until today. Since many crop circles are never reported, the actual number of crop circle events is expected to be considerably higher than indicated here.

counties of Wiltshire and Hampshire. The phenomenon has spread all around the world, with reports from the Netherlands, Germany, France, Spain, Italy, Bulgaria, Israel, the United States and Canada (many hundreds of formations in the last decade, see Figure 1-2), Russia, Japan, China, New Zealand, Peru—to name just a few.

Numerous people with different backgrounds have studied the phenomenon over the years. One of the pioneers, mentioned earlier, was Dr. Terence Meaden, meteorological physicist. Dr. Meaden visited almost all of the British formations from the late seventies until the early nineties. In those days, all of them consisted of single circles or a combination thereof, sometimes positioned randomly and sometimes symmetrically with respect to one another. Dr. Meaden suggested that the solution to the problem could be found in small, local whirlwinds of ionized air, which he called *plasma vortices.*

Halfway through the eighties, the number of British crop circles began to increase dramatically, to several dozens per year. At the same time formations appeared elsewhere in Europe, for example, in the Netherlands, where the first reported formation appeared in 1979. The public interest increased further when in 1990 the British circles started to transform into more complicated and increasingly sophisticated patterns, featuring rings and rectangular bars, such as the formations at Cheesefoot Head, Crawley Doens, and Alton Barnes. From the very beginning, these *pictograms* were carefully watched by Dr. Meaden and other researchers, such as Colin Andrews, Pat Delgado, and Busty Taylor. Since the late 1990s, the formations have developed into beautiful, spectacular, and incredibly complicated diagrams, which can be seen worldwide on calendars and postcards, in commercials, and in many books.

Not a Simple Hoax

ALONG WITH THE INCREASING NUMBER OF REPORTED FORMATIONS (SOME say on the order of 10,000 since 1976), the number of crop circle researchers has grown exponentially, with representatives in many countries. Public awareness and interest have increased, and so has the number of people who believe that the phenomenon can be explained as the work of incidental pranksters. "I saw it on TV. Those circles were just made by these two guys," or similar remarks, can often be heard when the controversial subject of crop circles is discussed. However, anyone willing to put some effort into a more in-depth approach will soon discover that it is not that simple at all.

The enormous dimensions and impressive complexity of the figures alone suggest that it is not a simple area of pursuit. For example, on July 7, 1996, at a stone's throw (no pun intended!) from the famous Stonehenge megaliths in south England, a formation of 151 circles appeared during broad daylight. The total formation was over 380 feet wide. (See Figure 1-3.)

There was a rumor that a pilot had flown over Stonehenge at about 5:30 p.m., and had not seen anything, yet a little more than half an hour later he

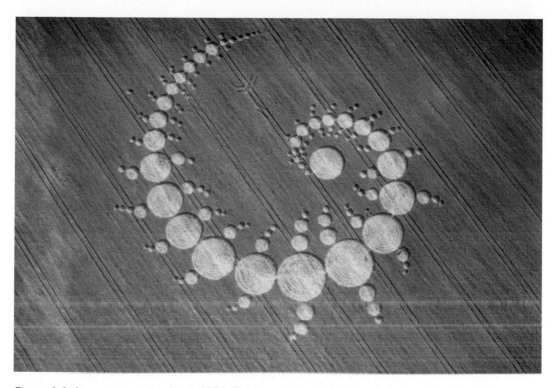

Figure 1-3. Stonehenge, England, 1996. Photograph © Steve Alexander.

flew back and discovered the magnificent formation. I suspected that this pilot could have been Busty Taylor, whom I had met a year before when he was lecturing in Amsterdam, so I decided to call him to inquire about the rumor. I found that it was not Taylor himself who had discovered the formation, but a friend. Taylor confirmed the story, relating that, "My friend has been looking at crop circles with me since 1988, and he knows what he is looking for. He flew over there at half past five in the afternoon, and he flew around Stonehenge seven times. The crop circles weren't there at half past five." David Kingston, ex-RAF pilot and now full-time crop circle researcher, told me that three independent witnesses had been found, all confirming the same event: The 1996 Stonehenge formation appeared within about half an hour, during broad daylight. A farm worker had also confirmed the absence of any shape in the field throughout the day, and a Stonehenge security guard had looked down into the field and had confirmed that there was nothing unusual there all day long. The many tourists at Stonehenge, as well as the many people driving over the adjacent highway, could have easily seen

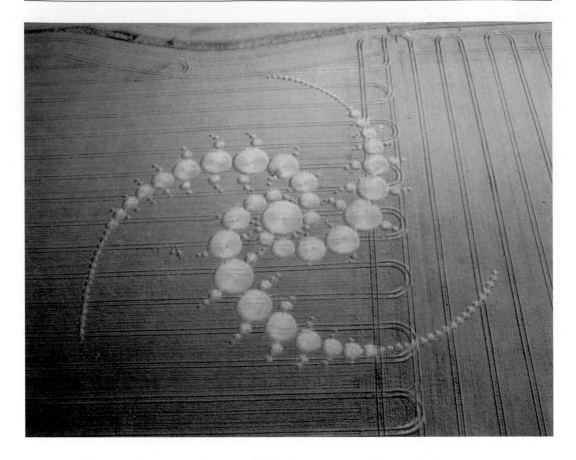

Figure 1-4. Windmill Hill, England, 1996. Photograph © Dr. Andrew King.

the formation in the adjacent field, which is in its entirety slightly uphill (I checked this personally in the summer of 2000). If it had been there all day, it is almost impossible that the formation remained unnoticed for so long. Hence, the explanation of a simple human hoax should be excluded.

Crop circle enthusiasts had hardly regained their breath after the appearance of this phenomenal pictogram, which was immediately called the "best crop formation ever," when three weeks later, on July 29, an even more spectacular formation appeared near Windmill Hill. This absolutely awesome formation contained the record number of 194 circles and had a total width of an impressive 375 feet. (See Figure 1-4.)

Often a presumed simple human joke can also be excluded for quite obvious reasons. An example is the *tree circle,* which was reported by the

Figure 1-5. Etten-Leur, Holland, 1997.

Czech researcher Petr Novák in 1994. It consisted of a circle 10 m in diameter, consisting of adult trees, which were bent at angles up to ninety degrees. In 1998 a similar report came from Butte (Montana, USA), where 150 acres of pine trees were completely flattened to the ground. No storms had been reported at the time whatsoever.

In 1997 a pictogram appeared in a Dutch carrot field. From the air, the formation did not look impressive at all (see Figure 1-5). It almost seemed as if the farmer had harvested some of the crop for personal use. The figure printed in the field consisted of an irregular kind of ellipse with a cross through it, plus a sort of rectangle, connected by a long pathway with a few sharp bends. Seen from the ground, the formation was one of the most bizarre I had ever seen. It was enclosed by high cornfields and was completely invisible from the road. The earth was very soft, which made it impossible to walk without leaving deep and clearly visible footprints. The field had been ploughed into long ridges, about twenty centimeters high, with

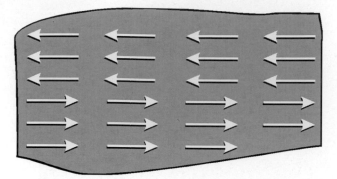

Figure 1-6. Carrot leaf lay.

the carrot plants growing on top. When I stepped on them, they immediately showed the traces of my own footprints, which were at least five centimeters deep, and crushed the carrot leaves into the ground. However, inside the formation, there were no footprints anywhere, and the carrot plants seemed completely untouched, although they lay withered against the ground, almost as if they had been cooked. It was quite a contrast compared with the surrounding plants, which were of a fresh green color, standing firmly upright.

But the most curious thing was the direction of the lay. In one half of the rectangle, the carrot leaves lay forward, while in the opposite half they lay backward (see Figure 1-6). On the imaginary boundary line separating the two halves, there was a long row of carrot plants of which roughly one half of the leaves had been flattened in one direction, while the other half of the leaves *of the same plants* had been flattened in the opposite direction. This can be seen in Figure 1-7. At the right the leaves are bent away from you; at the left they are bent toward you; and in the middle the leaves of a single plant seem to be "combed" in two directions, with a little tuft in the middle still standing upright.

It was clear that *no one had set foot inside this crop formation,* simply because of the lack of footprints. What was found, however, were various burn marks on the plants. In several places, the far ends of the carrot leaves were burned to ashes, and sometimes the entire leaf had been burned away (see Figure 1-8). Closer inspection of the stem revealed that it had been bent,

Figure 1-7. Lay of carrot leaves in Etten-Leur formation, Holland, 1997.

while its convex side only was covered with many tiny little dents, which seemed to be dehydrated. I checked many other plants throughout the field outside the formation, but none had similar marks on them, so it seemed unlikely to have been the effect of plant diseases or insects. It almost seemed as if the stem had been hit at one side by a shower of sparks, which had made it bend in the opposite direction.

Figure 1-8. Burnt carrot leaf.

Another remarkable finding was the pictogram in snow, which was created in the night between December 30 and 31, 1996. On a frozen and snow-covered field in the south of the Netherlands, after several days of hard frost, a circle (seven meters in diameter) with a superimposed cross was created, in which the snow had disappeared. And curiously enough, there were no foot-

Figure 1-9. Snow circle, Holland, 1996. Photograph © Robbert van den Broeke.

Figure 1-10. "Curtain" of standing stems along a tramline. Note how the downed stems have fallen in between the standing

prints leading to or from the formation. (See Figure 1-9.)

The observant crop circle visitor will also notice how plants growing at the very edge of the tramlines (the imprinted tracks of the tractor wheels) often remain upright, unlike the rest of the plants inside the crop circle. These stems create a sort of narrow "curtain" of upright stems, with a total length of many hundreds of meters (see Figure 1-10). Even more remarkable is the fact that many stems with their roots just a little further away from the tramlines are flattened just like the rest, and may actually fall over the tramlines, straight through the row of upright stems.

Another interesting characteristic can be found inside the numerous dozens of mini-

Figure 1-11. "Bird's nest" in 1997 Milk Hill formation. Photograph © Ron Russell.

circles that often surround the more elaborate pictograms. These accompanying circles, with a diameter of just a foot or two, often contain ornate works of art, such as stems densely intertwined into a three-dimensional toroid, with or without standing "tufts" in the center. Even more remarkable is the fact that these *bird's nests*, as they are called, often appear by many dozens, in locations that cannot be reached on foot without leaving obvious traces in the field. (See Figure 1-11.)

All these straightforward observations, in combination with the vast number of reported formations since the late seventies, should make one thing clear: Even if the crop circle phenomenon were the result of a worldwide hoax, it is certainly not a simple one!

The Dead Fly Enigma

ON JULY 17, 1998, THE DUTCH RESEARCHER JANET OSSEBAARD WAS CONfronted with a new crop circle–related mystery: numerous dead flies stuck on the seed heads of wheat plants inside a crop circle. Soon the same

Figure 1-12. Dead flies stuck on crop circle seedheads. Photographs © Janet Ossebaard (L) and © Dr. Uwe Engelmann (R).

observations were made by herself and by others in several other crop formations. The insects were firmly stuck with their tongues against the ears, and their legs and wings were spread out widely, as in a spasm. Pesticides could easily be excluded, because if that had been the case, dead flies would have been found throughout the field. Yet they were found solely inside the crop circles, and nowhere else. (See Figure 1-12.)

Some of the flies had literally exploded; their legs, pieces of their bodies and wings, and their heads were scattered over the seed heads. (A similar effect has been observed for many years in the stems of plants inside crop formations. These so-called *expulsion cavities* are an extreme case of swollen nodes, which will be discussed in more detail in Chapter Three.) Other flies, however, were still in a perfect state, and looked as if they could fly away any moment. Closer inspection revealed that most of them were nevertheless stone dead. However, some of them, although stuck to the seed heads just like the rest, were still alive, but severely stunned. After they were liberated from the plants, they recovered and flew away after a few minutes. Surprised by her observations, Janet collected some of the dead insects and sent them to an expert at the Natural History Museum in London. Here it was initially suspected that the effects of a fungus *(Entomophtora muscae)* were responsible for the dead insects, but after closer inspection it was concluded that this had not been the case. This was a phenomenon that had never been seen before, and no satisfactory answers could be given.

Curious Deposits

MANY TIMES, MYSTERIOUS SUBSTANCES ARE FOUND INSIDE CROP CIRCLES, such as jelly-like or powdery deposits on the plants and the soil. Several times, for example in 1996 near the city of Zutphen (the Netherlands) and in 1999 in Logan (Utah), a white, powdery deposit was found on the stems inside crop formations. After chemical analysis by the BLT research team in the USA, this white dust was identified as a high-purity silicon dioxide, SiO_2. Silicon dioxide (quartz) can be found anywhere on earth, but this time it had a remarkable appearance: under a microscope the dust appeared to consist of small, perfectly round spheres, with an average diameter around 50 μm (0.05 mm). Similar microscopic glass spheres may be obtained commercially. They are used in resin systems and plastics to lower their viscosity, in concrete to lower its specific mass, in abrasives, and for capillary absorption of fragrances or essential oils. However, there are also natural explanations for their occurence. Eolic airstreams may carry a fine dust which sometimes falls down during rainshowers (which causes "muddy rain," easily seen on the windscreen of your car). The combination of erosion and the (very small) solubility of silicon dioxide in water causes the dust to take the form of microspheres. Another form of silicon dioxide microspheres *(cenospheres)* is a waste product reclaimed from flyash which is produced during the coal burning process. Although the commerial availability of these glassy microspheres must be kept in mind, their presence in crop circles may indicate the involvement of intense heat, or somehow create a link with the higher atmosphere (see Figure 1-13.)

Other powdery deposits that have been found inside crop circles are magnesium oxide, and in particular magnetite (magnetic iron ore). In 1995, the American researchers William Levengood and John Burke published a scientific paper in which they reported ferriferous deposits on plants inside crop formations.[3] This marked the beginning of a continuous study during

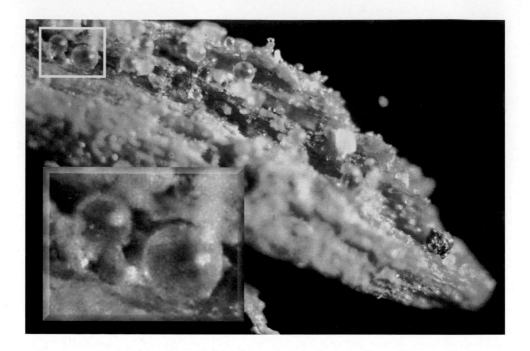

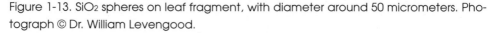

Figure 1-13. SiO_2 spheres on leaf fragment, with diameter around 50 micrometers. Photograph © Dr. William Levengood.

which the American researchers measured the magnetite concentration in the soil inside numerous crop circles all around the world. The macroscopic appearance of crop circle magnetite has been recognized as meteoritic in origin. This meteoritic dust drifts down daily from the atmosphere on earth, resulting in a nominal maximum concentration of 0.4 mg per gram of soil. Any higher concentration is remarkable. In crop circles, nevertheless, concentrations of 20 to even 250 mg per gram of soil have been found, which is more than a *six hundredfold* increase of the normal value. These findings perhaps indicate the presence of magnetic fields around crop circles, which attract meteoritic dust. It would also indicate that crop circles are somehow related to something in (or coming from) the atmosphere. However, these hypotheses are highly speculative, and the explanation remains a mystery to this day.

Another finding, which is sometimes reported, might also be caused by the presence of chemical substances inside crop circles. Sometimes, the patterns originally imprinted in the fields can still be seen during subsequent

Figure 1-14. Left: ground shot of a formation in Barbury Castle (UK), taken in the year 1999 (see also page 28). Right: photograph of the same field, taken exactly one year later. The "shadow" of the formation can still be seen in the field, because of a local growth disturbance (see photograph below). Photographs © Janet Ossebaard (top left) and © Bert Janssen (top right, bottom).

years in the form of biological changes to the crop. One example is illustrated in Figure 1-14 (left), which shows a ground shot of the "three bananas in a basket" formation of Barbury Castle, U.K., reported in the summer of 1999. Exactly one year later, Dutch crop circle researcher Bert Janssen visited the same location again and noted how a "shadow" of the formation could still be clearly seen in the field, with astonishing detail (Figure 1-14, right). The effect appeared to be created by a locally reduced growth of the plants (Figure 1-14, bottom).

Germination Anomalies

ANOTHER INTERESTING ANOMALY IS SEEN WITH SEEDS COLLECTED FROM crop circles during seed germination trials.[4] A germination trial is a standard test in biophysics, which determines the speed of seed germination and the growth rate of the young seedlings (a measure of seed quality). The seeds are put in special germination containers, and humidity, light, and temperature are carefully controlled. With each test, seeds collected from crop circles are compared to control seeds collected in the same field at the same time, but taken from the standing crop, far away from the imprints of the crop circles. Over 90 percent of many thousands of these tests revealed a most interesting biophysical anomaly. When a formation was formed in an immature crop, the seeds usually did not develop, or the growth of the seedlings was severely reduced. However, if a formation occurred in a more mature crop, the crop circle seeds seemed to be "energized," so that they grew at up to five times the normal rate.

At this point you should be aware that seed germination and the growth of seedlings are not casual, but well-known and well-documented processes. When humidity, temperature, light, and so on are known, there are well-established normal values for seedling length during the germination time. A fivefold deviation from these normal values is extraordinary. Whatever effect is causing this, it should be of great interest to all of us. If we could understand this mechanism, we could improve the seeds, the stock for future generations, increase farm yields, and therefore feed a lot more people from the harvest of our crops. (See Figure 1-15.)

Balls of Light

THROUGH THE YEARS, MANY PEOPLE HAVE CLAIMED TO HAVE WITNESSED the formation of a crop circle. Colin Andrews talks about a total of around seventy eyewitnesses so far. A number of these people have been interviewed, and their stories can be seen and heard on some of the crop circle videos that have appeared. Many other cases have been carefully documented, in particular by Dr. Terence Meaden.[5] According to these eyewitness reports, the

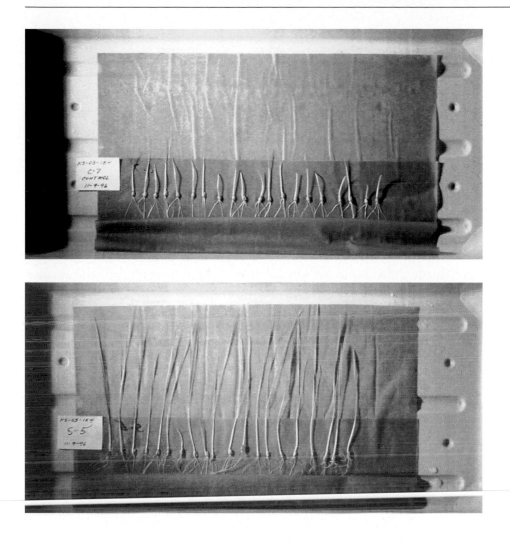

Figure 1-15. Germination anomalies. Top: 20 seeds taken 90 meters away from crop circle imprint, bottom: 20 seeds taken inside crop circle. Photographs: Dr. William Levengood.

crop is flattened by a sort of airstream. The eyewitnesses describe dust, sand, and other debris lifted up in the air in a rotating motion and falling back on top of the flattened crop in the crop circle, all in a matter of seconds. Dr. Meaden established several times that loose stems were lying on top of the flattened crop, in agreement with the eyewitnesses' statements. He also writes about "a large number of people" who all watched the formation of a crop circle together. "Suddenly the grass began to sway before our eyes and laid itself flat in a clockwise spiral, just like the opening of a lady's fan," according to these eyewitnesses. Lucy Pringle recently published several more eyewitness accounts, for example, the one by Gary and Vivienne Tomlinson:

> All at once the wind scooped us off the path into the cornfield. We took a great buffeting. It was very frightening. Looking down we saw a circle being formed around us. It only took a couple of seconds.[6]

Sound effects during the formation of a crop circle have been reported often, and sometimes resemble the humming sound you can hear near high voltage electricity cables. Other times, a hissing sound was reported, or a high-pitched whistling like a set of panpipes.

Dr. Meaden also reported optical effects directly related to the formation of a crop circle.[7] For example, around midnight of June 28, 1989, a big orange ball of light was seen descending into a wheat field in England. The witness saw the bottom go flat as it touched the ground and the crop, before disappearing after a single bounce, only a few seconds later. The next morning a ringed circle was found at the same spot. The Englishman Julian Richardson wrote on the Internet about a nighttime adventure in a crop field in 1992:

> Suddenly my attention was drawn to a light that had appeared from nowhere. It was a few hundred yards away and directly in front of us. As soon as I had registered its presence I alerted my colleagues. Amazed, we stood there gazing at this football-sized orange light as it hung motionless, about forty feet above the surrounding countryside. After an estimated five seconds the light began to slowly descend. Within another five seconds it had descended about ten feet and had faded into invisibility.[8]

Unidentified light objects have also been recorded on videotape several times, for example, by the Dutch researchers Foeke Kootje and Bert Janssen, the German von Dürckheim brothers, and the Englishman Steve Alexander. The latter, on July 26, 1990, shot the famous fifteen-minute video recording of an anomalous light object floating over a field near Stanton St. Bernard, England. In the background, one can see a farmer on a tractor noticing the ball of light as well. In fact, this man was identified a few days later. Immediately upon arriving home, he told his family about his strange observation. Not surprisingly, he was taken for a fool, until a few days later Alexander came along with his videotape.

According to Dr. Meaden, these observations are not only limited to England, but have also been reported from France, Japan, Australia, and the United States. And I can add my native country, the Netherlands, to that list. In 1996, I obtained a report from a sixteen-year-old boy named Robbert van den Broeke, who told me how he had witnessed the formation of a crop circle several times. When I discovered that his stories were similar to the statements of other eyewitnesses I had heard and read about, I obviously became interested. Just like many others, the boy also mentioned trembling air and crackling noises "as if you take off your sweater over your head," or, on another occasion, "as if you throw frozen French fries in hot oil." The creation of a crop circle, he says, occurred with one or multiple bouncing balls of light, spinning very rapidly through the crop "so that it almost resembled a fluorescent disk." Sometimes the balls had a white-bluish or white-pinkish color, or at other times more orange-like. According to the physical laws of electromagnetism, this could be an indication of varying temperature, while the trembling air around the balls could be the result of intense heat. After the formation is formed, in seconds, Robbert says, the light balls fade and disappear, "as if you switch off the television."

In 1998, Nancy Talbott (the "T" of the American research group BLT) visited the Netherlands during a lecture tour in Europe. She visited the western part of the province of Noord-Brabant, where each year many crop circles are reported, often accompanied by anomalous light phenomena. During a night watch, she was lucky enough to witness these anomalous lights, together with four other people. Soon after her extraordinary experience, she wrote her story on the Internet:

> The light display I witnessed . . . was really quite incredible. A very strong physical sensation preceded the display, a tingling which moved up my body toward my head, reaching quite intense levels by the time it reached my neck (to the point where I was very seriously looking for the door), then abruptly ceasing and the light display beginning, many, many lights, some balls just hanging in

the air, some driblets, some like flash-bulbs, huge blobs dropping down and hitting the patio floor, all aimed directly at the windows immediately behind which I and […] were sitting. The display would last for perhaps 30 seconds, then stop. Then 30 seconds to one minute would elapse and the tingling would start again, slowly rising up our bodies, reaching an intensity level at our necks which was close to uncomfortable, then, boom, it would stop and the light display would start again. This happened over an 11 minute period, from about 2 a.m. to 2:11 a.m., with somewhere between 5–7 of these light displays occurring.[9]

Knowing Nancy to be an intelligent, sober, and critical person, I believe her story, no matter how fantastic it seems. One of the reasons for my faith is that I already possessed other evidence that in fact these curious light balls had manifested themselves in this particular neighborhood. One year earlier I had visited the same region, after similar reports of flying balls of light. I was told how the balls of light had hit the roof shingles of a house at a height of about four meters, leaving clear burn marks on the painted wood. A little birdbox hanging on the front wall had also been hit. After I took it down, I saw how its metal roof showed undeniable perfectly round burn marks, with a diameter of about one centimeter. The fact that the burn marks were concentrated along

Figure 1-16 top. Birdbox showing circular burn marks on its roof, allegedly caused by "balls of light." The yellow arrows show that the burn marks are concentrated along the sharp edges of the metal roof, possibly indicating the involvement of electromagnetic forces. Figure 1-16 bottom. Close-up of birdbox roof. The coin has a diameter of 21 millimeters.

the sharp edges of the roof may indicate a possible electromagnetic character of the curious balls of light, as would be predicted by electromagnetic theory. (See Figure 1-16.)

Apart from direct eyewitness accounts, sometimes there are also circumstantial indications that balls of light might indeed be associated with the creation of crop circles. Through the years I have noticed several times how a narrow track of flattened crop led from the formations to the edge of the field. Sometimes there have been two of these tracks, one with the flattened crop directed toward the crop formation and the other with the crop flattened in the opposite direction, as if a small "something" had moved from the edge of the field into the formation, and back afterwards, flattening the crop during its course. These tracks were typically just a few centimeters wide (sometimes just a handful of stems), much narrower than the width of a human foot. The crop inside the tracks was neatly and accurately flattened, similar to the inside of the crop formation, unlike tracks left by people or animals. In the summer of 1998 a similar track was discovered near a circle in grass near the village of Hoeven in the Netherlands. The track led out of the crop circle, straight into a little adjacent canal. The tips of the grass stalks that made the track were bent and appeared dehydrated, not an unusual observation in crop circles. Interestingly, the stems were not flattened all the way down to the ground, but were rather bent halfway, so that the bottom of the track was still some twenty centimeters above the ground. This directly excluded a track made by a human or an animal. Perhaps this track was a leftover from a ball of light, flying out of the crop circle? (See Figure 1-17.)

Figure 1-17. Track of dehydrated grass, leading out of a crop circle. Perhaps caused by a "ball of light"?

Curious Events

As I have already said in the preface, during the study of crop circles one should take care not to reach premature conclusions or indulge in speculative arguments. For this reason, all crop circle–related phenomena I have shown so far are objective observations, all with references or clear photographs. However, many crop circle researchers have reported strange and incomprehensible events happening to them during their presence in the circles. Most crop circle books contain an abundance of these mysterious anecdotes. However, because most of these are single and uncontrolled events, experienced by individual people and often without a comprehensive report, it is very difficult to value their significance. A simple example: If someone notices that his watch is slow, he will have it fixed or change the battery and forget about it. When he notices the same thing when he is standing in a crop circle, he might very well be convinced that the battery was depleted by "circle powers." So one must be extremely careful coming to the correct interpretation, and only reach conclusions from carefully prepared experiments, not from accidental occurrences. Nevertheless, the abundance of strange and unexplained experiences by people visiting crop circles, and in particular the similarity of experiences by different people, is too conspicuous to be completely ignored. This insight is enhanced when weird things start to happen to *you*. I will therefore briefly report on some personal curious experiences, just for the reader's interest, and without concluding anything.

Failure of photographic gear in crop circles has been reported innumerable times, and falls perfectly in the category of slow watches that need a battery replacement. That is what I used to say for many years, until one day my own video recordings of a crop circle got corrupted too. I checked for trivial explanations but found none. In the same formation my Minolta 7000i produced only overexposed photographs—but only when I was standing inside the crop circles. The few I had taken while standing outside the circles were properly exposed. The camera worked perfectly for two years, until photographing another crop circle, when the electric motor winder got stuck (an often-reported problem in crop circles). Since then I have had no subsequent problems, except several occasions of strange black dots on photographs of crop circle sites, in particular on infrared film (another often-reported anomaly).

My watch has slowed down several times by a quarter of an hour or more on days I visited crop circles. It is a high-quality, ultra-accurate watch, which I usually adjust only twice a year: for daylight saving time and back.

I am thirty-eight, healthy, and a sound sleeper during eight of every twenty-four hours. Nevertheless, I do experience sleeping problems after visiting crop circles. Some nights, after a "circle day," I cannot fall asleep all night long and get up the next morning *not tired at all,* while other times I am so tired when I come home that I fall asleep on the couch before dinner. Is this just autosuggestion? Perhaps, but it would not explain why I once saw an entire bus full of people fall asleep just a few minutes after having visited a newly formed crop formation.

The funniest event that ever happened to me has become known as the story of the mouse. In 1997, I had taken samples for germination trials from a formation in Melick, the Netherlands, a total of about fifteen bunches of about twenty stems each. I also had collected control samples, far outside the formation. Each individual bunch was tied together and labeled. Due to lack of time, the material soon ended up as one big heap of straw on a table inside my garage. Several weeks later I got it out for the germination experiments. I arranged all the bunches on a table, and out of each seed head I pulled a single seed. When I arrived at the bunch of stems with the controls, my experiment failed immediately, even before I had the chance to plant the seeds in the germination containers. To my utter astonishment, I noted that nearly all seed heads of the controls had disappeared. I must have been staring at it for several seconds (with a not very intelligent look on my face), when I suddenly remembered seeing a mouse in the garage, a few days earlier. And indeed, underneath the table on which I had put the bunch with samples, I found a generous amount of empty seed heads, along with little mouse droppings. I realized that the mouse must have been nosing about in the bunch of wheat and somehow managed to eat only the control seeds. Not a single seed sampled from inside the crop circle had been touched! It reminded me of an experiment that was performed in the early nineties in England. Seeds sampled from a crop circle, with the same amount of seeds sampled from somewhere else in the same field, were used to bake two loaves of bread, simultaneously, in exactly the same manner. The ordinary bread tasted fine; however, the "crop circle bread" appeared to have a bad, sharp aftertaste. Since a mouse's sense of smell is much better developed than a human's, I could imagine that the mouse in my garage sensed that the seeds of the crop circle would taste bad and consequently had dinner with the controls only. Since then, I always hang my samples high up on the ceiling.

Don't Get Me Wrong

EVER SINCE I HAVE BECOME INTERESTED IN CROP CIRCLES, I HAVE BEEN approached many times for interviews, in particular by journalists and radio or television reporters. It is remarkable how many times, before you have even said a single word, people automatically stigmatize you as a crop circle *believer,* a person who *wants* crop circles to be a mystery, stubbornly defying mundane explanations. Several times, particularly on talk shows and similar happenings, other people participated in the discussions, playing the role of skeptical *nonbelievers.* They always brought up simple causes for the appearance of crop circles (human pranksters with planks and ropes being the most common, of course). After reading this chapter, you will understand that this approach is not particularly meaningful. It is important to be an objective observer, but as yet there are no satisfactory explanations for all my (and others') observations. And that is not a case of failure as a scientist, as has been suggested. On the contrary, it is a strong motivation to continue the research.

Notes

1. Pat Delgado and Colin Andrews, *Circular Evidence* (London: Bloomsbury Press, 1990).

2. G. T. Meaden, *Circles from the Sky, Proceedings of the 1st International Conference on the Circles Effect at Oxford* (Souvenir Press, 1991).

3. W. C. Levengood and John A. Burke, "Semi-Molten Meteoritic Iron Associated with a Crop Formation." *Journal of Scientific Exploration* 9, no. 2 (1995): 191–199.

4. W. C. Levengood, "Anatomical Anomalies in Crop Formation Plants," *Physiologia Plantarum* 92 (1994): 356–363.

5. See note 2 above.

6. Lucy Pringle, *Crop Circles, The Greatest Mystery of Modern Times* (Harper-Collins, 1999).

7. See note 2 above.

8. www.circlemakers.org/amber.html.

9. www.cropcircleconnector.com/archives/inter99/Hoeven99a.html.

Barbury Castle, England, 1999. "Three bananas in a fruit basket." One year later, the shape of this pictogram could be seen again in the field, as a result of locally reduced growth of the crop (see Figure 1-14).

Photograph © Janet Ossebaard.

Milk Hill, England, 2000. This photograph shows how crop circles integrate smoothly with their environment and are in perfect harmony with the landscape, despite their non-natural, intellectual design. The white horse was cut in the chalk hill in 1812 (and is hence not pre-historic, as sometimes thought). Photograph © Janet Ossebaard.

Milk Hill, England, 2000.

Photograph © Janet Ossebaard.

Swindon, England, 1999.

Photograph © Dr. Andrew King.

Windmill Hill, England, 1999.

Photograph © Dr. Andrew King.

Chapter 2

The Human Perspectives

The true character of the crop circle phenomenon is unknown to the public and is often erroneously ridiculed. In fact, crop circles are severely underestimated in their complexity by many, and, more interestingly, people seem to have formed very explicit opinions without knowing even the most basic facts. The different reactions of people to the crop circle phenomenon are therefore almost as interesting as the phenomenon itself, as will be shown in this chapter.

Believers, Thinkers, and Deniers

IT IS MY EXPERIENCE THAT THE REACTIONS OF PEOPLE WHO ARE CONFRONTED with the crop circle phenomenon for the first time, can be divided into three different classes: those of the Believer, the Thinker, and the Denier. The Believer will immediately accept everything you say. He or she listens fascinated to your stories, is excited but also happy about the news, and will enthusiastically start telling friends about it right away. Thinkers are more difficult to convince. These are mature, rational, and intellectual people. They come up with critical questions, suggest alternative and trivial explanations, and demand references. Nevertheless, the Thinker is certainly interested, although he or she will refrain from giving an immediate opinion. The Denier, however, is very different, and comes in two flavors: the Evil Denier and the Laughing Denier. The Evil Denier may evolve into an aggressive creature, who sets a personal goal to attack all this "crop circle garbage" as often and as much as possible. Some Evil Deniers are a little milder and limit themselves to just some remarks, such as: "Do me a favor will you, and stop that nonsense, please don't be ridiculous." The Laughing Denier, however, is never aggressive. The Laughing Denier laughs. "Ho-ho-ho, do you really believe that?" would be his or her first reaction. The Laughing Denier has a patronizing attitude and implicitly pretends to understand things much better than you do. He or she thinks that by the time you grow up, you will understand it too. A typical remark of a Laughing Denier would be: "Sure, crop circles, I guess they are made by Martians. Hey, can't you telepathically call them and ask if they will make a circle or two in my front yard, then I don't have to mow the lawn so often, ho-ho-ho." A similarity between the Evil and the Laughing Denier is that neither is willing to listen to you, and no reasoning seems to be possible with them. Without doubt this is related to an explicit lack of interest.

Obviously, the scenario sketched here is somewhat black and white, and in daily practice many combinations and variants exist. I know people who reveal many characteristics of the Believer, the Thinker, as well as the Denier, all at the same time. Without exception they will always make a silly remark as a reaction to the things I tell them, but nevertheless they show up on a regular basis to hear the latest news, look at the latest aerial photographs, or even report a new formation. Believers and Deniers often have very clear opinions, despite lack of (detailed) knowledge. The arguments they use are often erroneous, speculative, or based on inaccuracies. Nevertheless, this does not stop most of them from being absolutely convinced of how they believe things are. It is obvious that emotions and "gut feeling" play an important role. Fortunately, the amount of reference literature about crop circles is increasing, as you can see from the listing at the end of the book. Nevertheless, it takes a critical mind to distinguish the facts from the fiction.

The Crop Circle Expert

MANY PEOPLE THINK THAT A CROP CIRCLE EXPERT IS SOMEONE WHO CAN immediately distinguish a "real" crop circle (whatever it may be) from a man-made hoax. My opinion is that someone who judges the genuineness of a crop circle just by visual inspection is an amateur. Things are really not that simple, certainly not as long as we do not even know exactly what mechanism creates crop circles. Obviously, the experienced field researcher has developed an eye for indications of human activity, but since most of these could also be caused by the presence of early visitors, these observations can never be conclusive. Furthermore, the many so-called criteria that are in circulation, such as *broken* versus *bent* stems, a *circular* versus an *elliptic* circumference, the epicenter of the spiraling swirls concentric with the geometric center or off-center, and other "rules of thumb," are of little value. You don't need them anyway, because reliable conclusions can only be reached after extensive fieldwork and many hours of intensive laboratory work. If any anomalies or other interesting findings are found, it will probably take many more experiments with continuously adapted methods and careful reporting before we can come closer to the understanding of these observations. This is the process during which the researcher becomes an expert, and it is the only way to systematically unravel the crop circle mystery.

The Crop Circle Hoaxer

ANYONE CLAIMING THAT ALL CROP CIRCLES CAN BE EASILY EXPLAINED AS the work of human pranksters, or *hoaxers* as they are usually called, reveals that he does not know what he is talking about. However, this does not mean that no crop circles have been made by people. In England, there are several teams of crop circle hoaxers who have practiced a lot and developed great skill in the creation of crop formations with the aid of relatively simple tools. Most of the hoaxes are made in grain fields, but rarely in maize, carrots, potatoes, mustard, spinach, tobacco, grass, snow, or any other type of vegetation in which crop formations have appeared. There are many ways to make a hoaxed crop circle, varying from simple hand- or foot-stomping, through methods with planks and ropes (the method used by the well-known, self-proclaimed British hoaxers Doug Bower and Dave Chorley), garden rollers, or rotating PVC pipes. I am confident that even very complicated examples of crop formations that have been found over the years, in principle, could have been man-made. That is, as long as closer studies have not revealed any counterindications.

Since in many cases a careful (bio-)physical analysis is not performed, it is important to always keep one's options open. A plea such as: "This pattern is so complex, it *cannot* not be man-made!" is extremely dangerous. Professor Vincent Icke, a Dutch astronomer, once said to me: "Unscrew the back cover of your television set and take a look inside; then you will say the same thing: This cannot be man-made!" And he is right, of course. People are capable of many things, and I sincerely believe that anyone with the right drive and a little experience in geometry can develop working methods that allow the creation of very complex, perfectly symmetric crop formations. Nonetheless, there are an abundance of curious characteristics that have been discovered in crop circles time after time, which have yet to be reproduced by men. Scientific research has shown germination anomalies, cellular anomalies, intricate and well-structured lengthening of the nodes (the "nuckles" in the stems of corn-type plants), exploded nodes, burn marks, and even unnatural radioactivity, all of which cannot be the result of simple mechanical flattening. A crop circle is more than just a piece of flattened vegetation: It is accompanied by a considerable amount of unusual observations, far too many to simply dismiss the phenomenon as "caused by man," without further thinking.

Many people think that crop circle hoaxers are sober, rational persons, continuously leading the crop circle researchers (credulous and naive poor souls) by the nose. Skeptic articles in newspapers and magazines often create this image. In reality, however, crop circle hoaxers are often quite "esoteric." Many of them believe in a genuine crop circle phenomenon, and some are even convinced that they are an authentic part of it! They believe they are inspired by an unknown intelligence and perform their work in a sort of hypnotic state. The nonsober and nonrational approach of some crop circle hoaxers also becomes clear, for example, from the directions that are given on the "Make your own Circle" page I found on the Internet, where it is explained how a crop circle is made.[1] The recommended equipment consists of, besides logical material such as measuring tape, ropes, planks or a heavy garden roller, also "dowsing rods—these should be made of copper, and purchased from an expensive new age shop, or, in an emergency, a couple of bent coat-hangers will do." Step two of the instructions reads:

> Dowse potential location to establish earth energies. If a formation is located on a powerful ley-line, this will satisfy later tests for genuineness, and aid in curative effects, healings, orgone accumulation, angelic visions, benign alien abduction experiences, and

feelings of general well-being. WARNING — If the formation is situated contra-directionally to the flow of energy, this may result in the opposite effects; headaches, nausea, temporary limb-paralysis, aching joints, mental illness, deadly-orgone-radiation (DOR) exposure, demonic visions, negative abduction scenarios (memory loss, implant scarring, sore or bleeding anii, navels, and genitals, etc.), and general disillusionment.

One of the members of a group with the macabre name Team Satan wrote on the Internet:

> I truly believe that the circles we put down are genuine, and act to catalyze a whole host of other paranormal experiences. How else can we account for the many reports of anomalies associated with crop circle sites, not only from those who come to view and research the phenomenon, but also from the very people who create the circles?[2]

Here he refers to numerous accounts by crop circle hoaxers, who were confronted with curious light phenomena during their nightly circle-making adventures. In a press release they made at the end of the 1997 season, John Lundberg and Rod Dickinson wrote:

> Our crop formations are intended to function as temporary sacred sites in this landscape. Whilst constructing crop formations in the fields we have experienced series of aerial anomalies including small balls of light, columns of light and blinding flashes. All apparently targeting ourselves and our crop formations. We are not surprised by the numerous visitors who have reported a diverse assortment of anomalies associated with our artworks. These have included physiological effects, such as headaches and nausea, healing effects such as one report of a cure for acute osteoporosis, physical effects such as camera and other electronic equipment failure. We are certain that our artworks are subject to the attention of paranormal forces and act to catalyze other paranormal events.[3]

The current number of active hoaxers can only be estimated. Colin Andrews recently stated in a press release that eighty percent of the British formations are man-made. If you want to find such an estimate, you would have to examine a considerable amount of the total number of formations with solid, identical, and reliable methods, based on solid statistics. Performing such a test is not a trivial thing. Levengood has found unexplained anomalies in ninety percent of his experiments, which cannot be explained as the effects of mechanical flattening. This is quite a different number than that mentioned by Andrews, although Levengood's findings do not have to indicate that ninety percent of *all* crop circles would show these anomalies. I tend to believe that the assumed involvement of crop circle hoaxers is much exaggerated, but that is just a combination of gut feeling and an "educated guess." And it does not really matter. As long as we do not yet understand the observed anomalies, we have other things to worry about.

The Crop Circle Debunker

A CROP CIRCLE DEBUNKER DOES NOT BELIEVE THERE IS ANYTHING UNEXplained about the crop circle phenomenon, is convinced that it can all be simply explained as the work of humans, and does not leave any opportunity unused to bring that news out in the open. So the debunker is not the same person as the hoaxer, although combinations do exist: debunkers who create crop circles themselves in order to support their point of view. The strategy in that case is usually as follows: A piece of crop is flattened, by ordinary means, and somehow it is arranged that crop circle "researchers" investigate this man-made creation and come up with statements about its genuineness. As soon as somebody declares the formation as "not made by men," the debunker reveals that the formation was in fact man-made, and then concludes that the crop circle phenomenon is just the work of humans and nothing more. This approach is completely ill-founded, and similar to showing an imitation pearl to some arbitrary people in the street. When one of them says that the pearl is real, you say this proves that real pearls do not exist. Yet, amazingly, this approach has been used over and over again by news reporters. However, anyone can come forward with a statement about the genuineness (or lack thereof) of a crop circle, and in doing so will definitely reveal his or her qualities as a researcher. But how can such statements possibly be related to the authenticity of the crop circle phenomenon in its entirety? As always, the complexity of crop circles is much underestimated, and these attempts to reach conclusions without evidence can be dismissed.

Some have even spent serious amounts of money to prove that crop circles are just human pranks. In 1998, the American television station NBC sponsored a costly project and had the well-known crop circle hoaxers John Lundberg, Rod Dickinson, and Wil Russell fly over to the southernmost tip of New Zealand to produce an elaborate hoax before running cameras. The formation looked good from an aerial photograph, but as you will understand by now, that is not the main issue. It is unfortunate that the formation was made secretly, almost as far away as possible from active crop circle researchers, while the pictogram was cut off the field almost immediately after it had been finished. No samples were taken for biophysical analysis, not a single established researcher was allowed to even inspect the lay of the crop. So what did they prove? Nothing. If anyone really feels the urge to prove that the most complex crop formations can be made by men in a single night, why does nobody accept the challenge to duplicate one of the best formations that have appeared earlier, such as the Milk Hill Koch fractal of 1997, or the 1996 Windmill Hill formation? It could be a joint undertaking by crop circle researchers and crop circle hoaxers, performed in public, and it would be a most interesting project for everybody, independently of the outcome. It would also be the perfect scenario for an exciting and informative media show, so finances should not have to be a problem either. Moreover, if the project were performed in the fields of Hampshire or Wiltshire in England, you could save the costs of the plane tickets to New Zealand as well.

Debunkers often criticize research methods. Despite the many premature claims that have been made in the past by crop circle fanatics, this criticism is not always well founded. It is a normal course of matters, especially in the early stages of research on a new phenomenon, that certain research criteria are not well defined yet. The continuous adapting and improving of experimental methods is a normal process, which indicates progress and not failure. Of course, a critical approach, objectivity, and the honesty of the researcher remain essential. But sometimes the activities of debunkers can almost be considered sabotage. There was an unfortunate incident of sprinkling iron filings on the flattened stems inside a crop circle, after which the chemical analyses that were performed on the plants and the soil were ridiculed. This can be compared with deliberately exchanging blood samples during the development of a vaccine and accusing the researchers of ignorance when the results appear to be inconsistent. Activities of this kind have no value, nor will they serve to enfeeble the mysteries around the crop circle phenomenon. All this shows, really, is that some debunkers are apparently quite intent to prove their point.

A virtuous debunker, instead, would focus on well-documented observations and experiments, and should not only try to find flaws in the work of others. He or she should also repeat the experiments and compare results, by mutual arrangement with the original researchers. Those who believe that this would be too much work or lack the proper scientific background to perform the experiments correctly should refrain from any comment. This is the only way in which progress can be made in the scientific world. If scientists, through the ages, had had the same mentality as some crop circle debunkers of today, we would probably still dress in bear skins.

On the other hand, sometimes the criticism of debunkers is justified. There are many self-proclaimed crop circle researchers who do not understand what they are doing, draw premature conclusions, publish their incorrect findings in magazines, books, and on the Internet, and in doing so cover up the essentials of the crop circle phenomenon. The flaws in their reasoning can be extremely disturbing, and many readers will contemptuously put these articles aside without paying attention to the basic message, which may very well be built on correct insights. Despite their good intentions, the work of these so-called researchers can have a very bad effect on the public opinion about crop circles. It does no harm when this is spoken out loud. So some debunkers do contribute to crop circle research, because they keep the critical researchers sharp, and they compensate for the many overenthusiastic crop circle worshippers.

Ockham's Razor

Several opinion surveys can be found on the Internet about the statement: "Crop circles are simply the work of human pranksters." On average, more than one half of the respondents support this statement, whereas the remainder believe that something more must be happening.

These numbers are probably not very representative of the general public. It is likely that most participants in the polls would have not found the related Web sites if they were not trying to find crop circle–related information and hence already had a particular interest in the crop circle phenomenon. Without doubt, this self-selection biased the outcome. My impression is that today about half of the population does not even know what a crop circle is, while less than ten percent would take the phenomenon seriously. The persistence of the explanation "simply the work of human pranksters" is probably related to the principle known as Ockham's razor: If two theories explain the facts equally well, then the simpler theory is to be preferred. The recently deceased American scientist Carl Sagan propagates this principle in his latest (and last) work, *The Demon-Haunted World: Science as a Candle in the Dark.* According to Sagan, it is crucial to try to keep every explanation for an arbitrary observation as simple as possible. This viewpoint brings nothing new; it is a well-known dogma in the scientific world. However, in my opinion, Albert Einstein phrased the principle considerably better: "All theories should be made as simple as possible—but not simpler." This statement expresses exactly why I cannot convince myself that crop circles must be solely attributed to human pranksters. The hypothesis does not explain the facts well at all. It is indeed a simple, but not an adequate explanation. It is an explanation full of inconsistencies that need to be addressed in detail before this hypothesis can be a candidate for Ockham's razor.

Emotional Proof

ANOTHER STATEMENT THAT CAN OFTEN BE HEARD IN CROP CIRCLE–RELATED discussions (and also other discussions, of course) is: "I can only believe something after it has been proven." Scientists and people with scientific backgrounds frequently make this statement. And it seems obvious, certainly for a scientist, not to accept everything without thinking, but to request proof for whatever is stated. But if you think about it carefully, things are not always so simple as they seem. The issue has been phrased in a saying from John and Lynn St. Clair Thomas: "For those who believe, no proof is necessary; for those who do not believe, no proof is possible."

At this point, perhaps it makes sense to think about the question: What is proof? The *Oxford Dictionary of Current English* defines *proof* as "evidence, that is sufficient to show that something is a fact." The requirements this evidence has to fulfill, however, will differ from case to case and from person to person. Some will be perfectly happy with a simple statement, just because they trust the person who makes the statement. Someone else might not be satisfied before an extensive analysis is presented, taking into account all relevant aspects and completely following all written and unwritten rules of Western science. In practice it turns out that the latter is not always simple. When we deal with an apparently controversial subject like crop circles, even unambiguous findings, published in scientific and peer-reviewed journals, have been dismissed by skeptics as being the result of inaccurate procedures, not enough data, and a wild imagination. It has even been suggested that such experiments are deliberately manipulated to support the underlying theories. Besides the fact that such an unsupported allegation is of no value, it is clear that an attack on any scientific experiment can be camouflaged by suggesting alternative explanations. The criterion of accepting evidence, however, should not be that one cannot think of any possible alternative. Apparently it is also crucial that the explanation given be plausible.

From this point of view, *proof* is a far more emotional concept than one would expect. A scientific article, for example, is considered plausible as long as it follows the rules of science and the common, known theories. Nevertheless, nearly all of these theories are only accepted because professors at universities teach them, or because we can read about them in scientific books. Strictly speaking, it is largely a matter of *trust* that all of us, scientists included, have so much confidence in these theories and physical laws. One could object to this statement by saying that whenever someone doubts their validity, all theories of physics may be verified (or falsified) by checking their consistency with observations, measurements, and other known theories. Which is true, of course. But do we always do that? No, of course not. No scientist lives long enough to verify the reliability of all the theories he or she uses. And even if someone did, the rules of reasoning that would be used in order to perform such verifications also come from a book. The conclusion is clear: The confidence we have in our scientific methods is largely based on trust. It is directly related to the *faith* we have in them and the *feeling* that they must be correct. And there is nothing wrong with that. In fact, this "feeling" is usually referred to as *physical insight,* which often distinguishes a good scientist from a more moderate one. Still, as a consequence, scientists can only *believe* that the theories they are familiar with, and which are used by them, their colleagues, and their many predecessors, are indeed correct. In light of this, however, saying "I only believe things if they have been proven" loses all meaning, and would be equivalent to saying: "I only believe things when I believe them." Or, in other words: Not believing is simply a matter of not *wanting* to believe, which leads us right into the definition of an "open mind"—or actually the lack thereof.

However, those of you who do not agree with this viewpoint and still feel the need for unambiguous scientific evidence before you are willing to accept the curious character of crop circles, should not put this book aside at this point. In the next chapter, solid scientific evidence will be presented, which proves that crop circles are indeed made by the mysterious balls of light introduced in Chapter One.

Stay Alert

HUMAN CROP CIRCLE MAKERS SOMETIMES COME FORWARD WITH APPARently very credible stories, which seem to take the edge off even the most impressive crop circle appearances and the most intriguing anecdotes about the phenomenon. Sometimes it is tempting to accept the trivial explanations they present ("We made this pictogram and there is nothing mysterious about that") and forget about all the rest. After all, accepting this simple explanation also takes the incredible burden of uncomprehended side effects off your shoulders. If hoaxers created these complex pictograms, then it is obvious to assume that all the reported anomalies must be the result of a misunderstanding, inaccurate procedures, or just something else, which can probably be explained too. I have to admit that even I sometimes start to doubt when I read the articles on the Internet written by crop circle hoaxers. Their story seems so obvious. Until ... you find that they sometimes pretend to know more than they actually do. In an interview with the American researcher Michael Lindemann on October 27, 1996, the well-known British crop circle hoaxer Rod Dickinson said that the spectacular formation near Stonehenge (July 7, 1996) had been created by mechanically flattening the crop with planks and ropes.[4] It was allegedly done by three men in two hours and forty-five minutes, in the night before the day it was found. Despite the many counterarguments, I was initially willing to consider this statement. However, later in the interview, when he explained how the formation had been made, Dickinson made a mistake.

> You start with the large central circle, which is placed right next to a tram line. People asked why [the formation] had the large central circle, which is a little out of place in a Julia Set. Simple. To avoid damaging surrounding crop, you have to have a large central area already laid down, from which you can measure out diameters to other parts of the formation. After making the first circle, they measured out a work line for the rest of the formation. This is how the spiral was made, drawing portions of the arc from different center points inside that first circle, using a tape measure. You keep moving the center point around that first circle, and lengthen the tape for each new part of the arc.

Despite this apparently intellectual plea, the exposition is not correct. A simple analysis of an aerial photograph, shown in Figure 2-1, shows that the "work line," as Dickinson called it, was definitely not constructed from the large central circle. In fact, the work line consisted of three circular segments, of which only one had its center in the central circle. The other two had their centers on a tramline and not in the central circle, as Dickinson said. His suggestion that the entire work line was constructed from the center circle was hence incorrect. This is not a theory, it is not an assumption, it is a fact. The remark about "drawing parts of the work line from different positions inside the large center circle" even reveals some ignorance. Since the central circle's diameter is much smaller than the span of the work line, this would have no visible effect on the final result. My conclusion is that Dickinson was less well informed about this alleged hoax than he wanted to pretend. It is another example showing that the crop circle world is tricky, and that one should take care not to accept any statement without critical thinking.

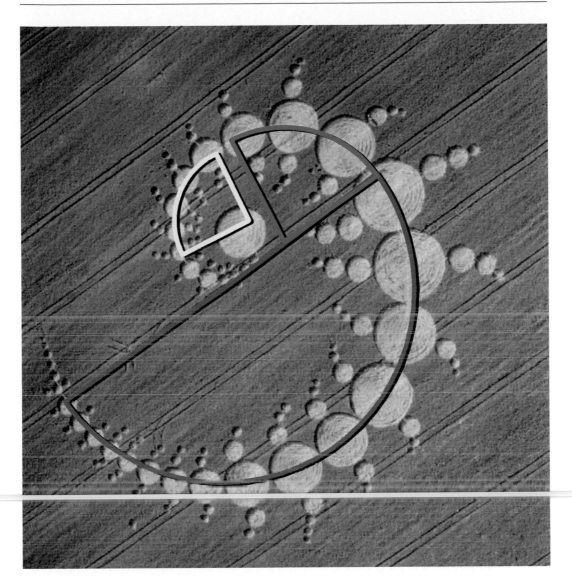

Figure 2-1 Analysis of the 1996 Stonehenge pictogram. The central "work line" or "back-bone" of the formation consists of three circular segments, one of which has its center in the large central circle, while two others have their centers on the tramline. Photograph © Steve Alexander.

The Press

MANY IDEAS AND STORIES CIRCULATING ABOUT THE CROP CIRCLE PHE-nomenon are inaccurate, or even completely wrong. One of the reasons, without doubt, is the prejudiced and often little accurate information that is spread by some newspapers, magazines, radio, and television. Despite lack of appropriate knowledge, some journalists and television reporters do not hesitate to present rumors, vague suspicions, or even personal opinions as solid and generally acclaimed facts. The impact of these statements on the public is overwhelming. In 1996, after a brief but informative and objective documentary about Dutch crop circles, the newscaster spoiled the show by saying: "Also in the north of Holland new crop circles were discovered—and immediately unmasked. Apparently, a farmer had seen a helicopter at night, flying in circles above the field, exactly on the spot where the next day the new crop circles were found." Such a remark does not testify to profound thinking. The mere suggestion that a helicopter could produce anything even slightly resembling a crop circle makes it clear that the newscaster had never seen one in real life. But the effect of his words was overwhelming. I cannot recall how many times since then I was told, "But I thought they solved that—weren't crop circles caused by helicopters?" The simple fact that the media apparently have such a strong influence on the public implies a severe responsibility for all news reporters, and it is my opinion that it would be good if they were a little more careful with what they say and write.

More amiss are cases in which journalists write personal attacks, rather than general criticism on crop circles and the activities around them. It is remarkable that these attacks are often done without any reason, that they are not based on clear or verified facts, and often are needlessly aggressive. Such attacks have happened to me several times. I can assure you that it is highly curious when you read an article about yourself, written by someone whom you have never met, who apparently does not know anything about the crop circle phenomenon, and who publicly writes that you say things that you would not even *think*. Journalists have even called me an idiot and cast doubt on my academic titles. The best thing one can do in these cases is completely ignore it. The few times I have spent effort on writing a comment, clarifying the matter, and pointing out the inaccuracies in the articles, I haven't received an answer back. However, most personal interviews I have done over the years were pleasant events, resulting in truthful articles. And even if interviews started badly, they almost always came out right. Several times I have had journalists come to my home with sulky faces, because their boss wanted them to make a crop circle documentary, which they thought was completely ridiculous. "We don't have much time," they used to say as soon as they entered my house. Typically, they left many hours later, sometimes completely flabbergasted, and always loaded with photographs, articles, and notes. And I still have regular contacts with many of them.

On the other hand, sometimes it does not work out. This is probably related to the unmasking game some reporters like to play, in which you have to play the role of victim right from the beginning. The goal of the unmasking game is to publicly reveal your ignorance as a "crop circle expert." As an example, I was once contacted by a commercial TV station and asked if I wanted to collaborate on a documentary about crop circles. I accepted and arrived for the interview a few days later. It was inside a giant crop circle that had been found a few days earlier. Initially, some basic questions were asked.

"Is this a simple natural phenomenon, you think?"

"Not likely. The design is too complex and unlike anything else we see in nature."

"Could it be man-made?"

"Of course."

But the interview soon soured. The reporter could not accept the fact that I had studied the phenomenon for so many years and still could not come up with an explanation. "You should have some idea by now," he repeated. His initial, apparently feigned ignorance gradually decreased as he more and more tried to force me into making explicit pronouncements in terms of extraterrestrial communication attempts, Gaia and Mother Earth, and other metaphysical explanations. My avoidance of dogmatic statements clearly frustrated the director of the crew. After a while, a reporter from another television station approached us and tried to speak to me, but was immediately led away by one of my interviewers, with the words "Can I talk to you privately for a second?" At the end of the interview, after I had to act before the camera as if I were investigating a wheat stalk, the final climax was set into motion: Before the running cameras I was confronted with three young men, who were presented as the creators of the formation. They had done the job in collaboration with the landowner. I imagine my interviewers saw the newspaper headlines before their minds' eye: "Crop Circle Expert

Unmasked, So-Called Scientist Duped." However, contrary to the ideas the television producers may have had, I had already been informed about this hoax long before they were, by one of my crop circle colleagues. Moreover, it has always been my strict habit never to say a word in public about genuineness of crop circles, and even less this time, for obvious reasons.

The TV guys were not happy with my reaction at the moment of the "grand finale," when I was introduced to the hoaxers. (I smiled and said something like: "Nice work, guys, I bet you didn't get much sleep that night!") They disappeared without even saying good-bye. But the real surprise came when I watched the documentary on television a few months later.

"Could it be man-made?"

"Not likely. The design is too complex . . ."

The video-editing was followed by a shot of young men stomping down a piece of crop at night with lots of laughter. At such moments it is amusing to realize that I pay money for a television license.

After this hoax, which had been given extensive attention in the media, many journalists and television reporters continued to contact me and still seemed to be sincerely interested in the genuine crop circle phenomenon. This confirmed my impression that sometimes the media also treat the crop circle phenomenon as something serious. Which is good for a simple reason: Regardless of the origin of crop circles, even if one day, despite all, it will appear to be the best joke in human history, the duty of the media is to inform the public with facts and not to invent the stories themselves.

Notes

1. www.circlemakers.org/guide.html.

2. This statement was originally made on www.geocities.com/SoHo/3671/index.html. Later this site was moved, and the statement appeared somewhat modified on www.circlemakers.org/press.html.

3. www.circlemakers.org/press.html.

4. www.circlemakers.org/la2.html.

The famous "Spiderweb" of Avebury, England, 1994.
Photograph © Dr. Andrew King.

Avebury, England, 1994. Close-up photograph of the "Spiderweb."
Photograph © Dr. Andrew King.

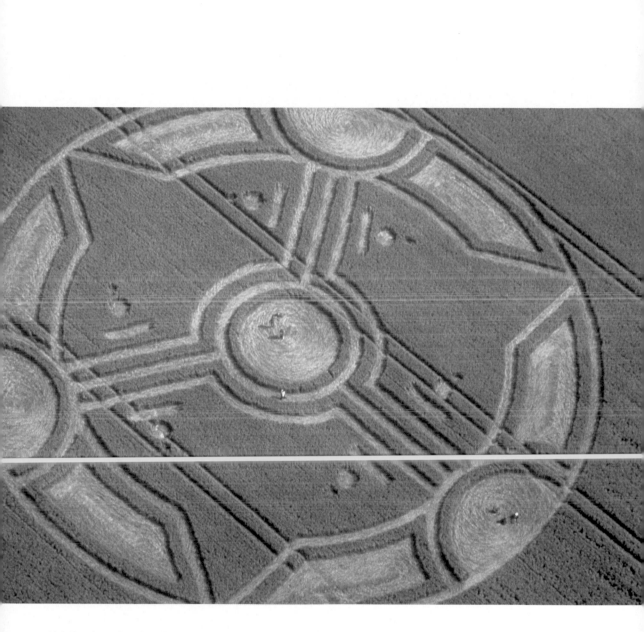

Liddington Castle, England, 1999.

Photograph © Ron Russell.

The magnificent Avebury Trusloe, England, formation of 2000. The figure resembles the interference pattern as caused by small, concentric circles on a computer screen, known as the "moiré effect" and was therefore nicknamed the "Moiré formation."
Photograph © Bert Janssen.

Pole shot of the formation in Avebury Trusloe, England, 2000. Here it can be seen clearly how the entire pattern was constructed from straight lines only. Photograph © Bert Janssen.

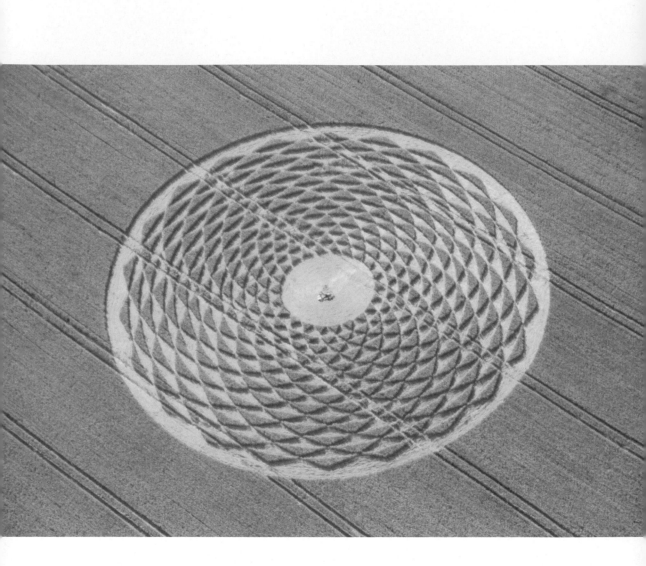

The breathtaking "Mandala" of Woodborough Hill, England, 2000, made out of 308 triangles of standing crop. Considered by many as the best formation ever.
Photograph © Bert Janssen.

Pole shot of the Woodborough Hill formation, England, 2000.

Photograph © Janet Ossebaard.

East Kennet, England, 1999.
Photograph © Ron Russell.

Chapter 3

The Scientific Perspectives

Ever since the first crop circles appeared they have been examined by many people in all sorts of ways. Some of the methods used were scientific, that is, following the rules prescribed by Western science; others were not, although most of the findings have been presented as "results of scientific research on crop circles." Scientific research, however, is something that requires special skills, usually as a result of intensive study. This does not mean that it is always difficult to understand. However, certain rules must be followed strictly. This chapter discusses the most important findings from scientific methods, varying from mathematical analysis of the designs, through biophysical tests, to reproducible measurements of other physical anomalies.

Hawkins's Theorems

PERHAPS THE MOST OBVIOUS SCIENTIFIC INVESTIGATION THAT CAN BE PERformed, when one is confronted with the intriguing shapes that crop circles can take, is a geometric analysis of the symbols. This was the approach followed by Dr. Gerald S. Hawkins, former chairman of the astronomy department at Boston University. Hawkins was probably the first person who unambiguously demonstrated that crop circles are much more than just some arbitrarily sized and randomly positioned patterns in the fields. After reading the bestseller *Circular Evidence,* in which an extensive overview was given of all British crop circles for the period 1978–1988, Hawkins analyzed all formations presented in this book.[1] In those early years the pictograms still had simple shapes: single circles, multiple circles in a pattern, and circles with concentric rings around them. All diagrams were put through a straightforward mathematical analysis, during which the proportions of the circle diameters and the areas inside the rings were determined. A total of twenty-five pictograms were taken into account.

Hawkins discovered that the resulting ratios revealed a strong correspondence to the white keys on a piano keyboard. The exact background of his analysis is given in Appendix A of this book. In simple terms it boils down to the fact that the white keys on a piano keyboard can be logically related to the ordinal numbers 0, 2, 4, 5, 7, 9, 11, and 12. The black keys can be represented by the numbers 1, 3, 6, 8, and 10. When Hawkins determined the geometrical ratios from the individual pictograms, he discovered that all of these corresponded to *integer* numbers. This fact in itself was remarkable, because arbitrarily sized circles would most often result in broken numbers (for example, 2.372 ...). However, the fact that each of the derived numbers was part of the series mentioned earlier, and hence directly corresponded to the white keys of a piano keyboard, was astonishing. Hawkins's findings are represented in Figure 3-1.[2] All possible proportional numbers *n*, defining the so-called *diatonic ratios,* are put along the horizontal axis, while the vertical axis indicates the number of times that each particular value of *n* was found.

It can be seen immediately that the yellow bars are not spread randomly along the horizontal axis, but seem to cluster around those positions where *n* equals 0, 2, 4, 5, 7, 9, 11, and 12. Most interestingly, not a single occurrence of one of the numbers 1, 3, 6, 8, or 10 was found, which would indicate a black key. The probability that this would be just a coincidence was calculated at 1 in 400,000, that is, completely negligible. It has been suggested that Hawkins's findings could be a consequence of simple human construction methods, for example, the use of

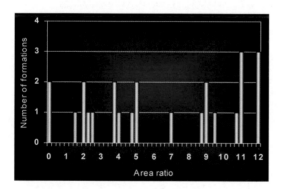

Figure 3-1. Hawkins's analysis. For 25 crop formations geometrical ratios of individual elements were determined, and represented by the diatonic number *n*, shown horizontally between 0 and 12, at intervals of 0.25. The number of "matches" for each value of *n* is shown on the vertical axis.

a measuring stick of fixed length. This would then automatically result in the determined proportions. This, however, is not the case, as will be explained in the following pages.

Music

THE PROPORTIONS OF THE ACOUSTIC FREQUENCIES CORRESPONDING TO A musical scale are such that the resulting combination of tones is pleasant to our ears. Any slight detonation of the pitch of one of the tones is usually heard immediately as a "false note." Consequently, one could suggest that the diatonic ratios determined by Hawkins are a prerequisite for *geometric harmony,* related to the human perception of sound. Following this concept, a logical follow-up of Hawkins's work (actually a sort of reverse engineering approach) was performed many years later by the Englishman Paul Vigay. Vigay transformed the geometrical patterns into acoustic sounds with the aid of a computer program. Although the exact algorithm he used is unknown to me, I imagine that the geometrical proportions of the crop circle patterns may be transformed by a computer into diatonic ratios, which can then be used to generate chords on a synthesizer. During a crop circle symposium in Glastonbury, England, in 1998, Vigay played a couple of melodies that had been produced by his computer program. It was a surprising experience. The melodies sounded very peculiar, unlike anything else I had ever heard or could even think of, but were without doubt very "harmonic" and certainly pleasant to listen to, in some sense. It was a sort of music that awoke your curiosity and made you want to listen longer to it. Isn't this exactly the hard part of composing music? Interestingly, the same computer program did not manage to produce anything similarly pleasing from man-made hoaxes. However, despite the interesting results demonstrated by Vigay, his findings can only be appreciated when the exact algorithm he used is known. The fact that a computer program produces "nice" music from some diagrams and "ugly" music from diagrams obtained from allegedly man-made formations is not interesting in itself, as long as one does not understand *why* this happens. Nevertheless, given the findings of Hawkins, Vigay's approach is creative and interesting, and definitely deserves more investigation.

Hidden Math

IN 1996, IN THE MAGAZINE *Science News,* HAWKINS REPORTED ANOTHER curious event.[3] His findings concerning the diatonic ratios were related to a total of four theorems he had formulated. These four theorems could be represented graphically by fitting three straight lines, an equilateral triangle, a square, and a hexagon between separate circular elements of pictograms (see Figure 3-2). Theorem I described the relative positions of three single circles, while theorems II–IV described the proportions of circles and their surrounding rings. Hawkins had discovered that between a central circle and a surrounding ring one could often exactly fit a triangle (theorem II), a square (theorem III), or a hexagon (IV).

Additionally, Hawkins had defined a fifth, general theorem, from which the other four could be derived. In other words, the first four theorems turned out to be special cases of the fifth one. Hawkins did not publish this fifth theorem; instead, he challenged the readers of the magazines *Science News* and *The Mathematics Teacher* to derive this unpublished fifth theorem from the four others. There were no correct responses, until in the summer of 1996 a crop formation appeared, which turned out to be an exact representation of Hawkins's "unknown" fifth theorem. It seemed as if only the anonymous circle creators knew how to successfully respond to Hawkins's challenge.

Despite crop formations having evolved into extremely complex patterns,

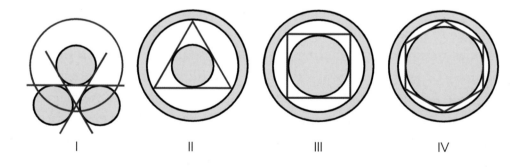

I II III IV

Figure 3-2. Hawkins's Theorems.

they still reveal an abundance of diatonic ratios. However, finding Hawkins's theorems in today's crop formations doesn't have as much significance as it had in the early days. Since Hawkins has published his findings several times, anyone with a little understanding of basic mathematics can design (and construct) crop circles based on Hawkins's theorems. Nevertheless, one may wonder how many people would go through the trouble of all the extra work, particularly because it is not at all guaranteed that anyone would notice the advanced design of such a formation, because the diatonic ratios are sometimes hidden deeply inside the diagrams. A poignant example is a pictogram that appeared in 1998 in a field of wheat near the city of Oud-Beijerland, Holland. (See Figure 3-3.)

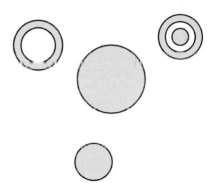

After a first analysis of a field diagram made by my fellow researchers Nancy Polet and Roeland Beljon, I discovered that this pictogram was by no means a collection of arbitrarily positioned circles and rings. It turned out that the pictogram had the remarkably large number of *six triple tangent lines*, that is, straight lines exactly touching the edges of three different circular elements (see Figure 3-4).

Figure 3-3. Oud-Beijerland, Holland, 1998.

The diagram almost seemed to be an advanced derivative of Hawkins's first theorem. Apparently, both the dimensions of all elements of the pictogram, as well as their exact relative positions, had been chosen with great care. However, not just the position of the elements with respect to each other, but also the pictogram's position in the field was not accidental. This fact was revealed when I discovered that some of Hawkins's theorems connected the pictogram to the position of

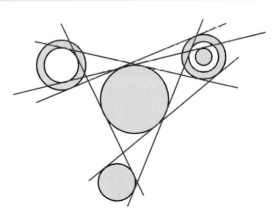

Figure 3-4. Six triple-tangent lines in the Oud-Beijerland formation.

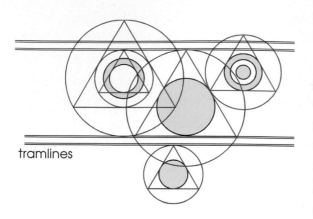

tramlines

Figure 3-5. Hawkins's theorems, related to the position of the pictogram elements with respect to the tramlines.

the tramlines in the field, as indicated in Figure 3-5.

You will notice that an equilateral triangle can be drawn around the central large circle of the pictogram. When another circle is drawn around this triangle, it appears that it exactly touches the upper tramlines in the diagram. The same exercise can be performed on the inner edge of the ring in the left of the pictogram. As you can see, the circle around the equilateral triangle perfectly touches the tramlines as well. And here the game can be repeated: When you draw a new triangle around the outer circle and add a new circle around this triangle, it exactly touches the bottom tramlines. Moreover, the single circle at the bottom fits in a triangle with surrounding circle that touches the tramlines at the bottom of the diagram. The circle with the concentric ring at the right of the pictogram does not seem to be related to any of the tramlines. Nevertheless, after drawing an equilateral triangle around the outer edge of the ring, the resulting circumscribing circle exactly touches the edge of the pictogram's central circle.

Now, could this all just be a coincidence? The answer seems to be highly unlikely, particularly when one realizes that the examples I have shown have been similarly discovered literally thousands of times in other pictograms. But the adventure has not yet ended. Until now, it has been shown that the positions of the elements with respect to each other were carefully chosen so as to obtain six triple tangent lines. Moreover, the position and the size of the pictogram itself were also chosen carefully with respect to the tramlines. However, an analysis of the four basic individual elements of the pictogram (two circles, a ring, and a circle with a concentric ring) shows that these also obey Hawkins's rules, as can be seen in Figure 3-6.

A copy of the small circle at the bottom has been drawn inside the large central circle. The two circles include an equilateral triangle, obeying

Hawkins's second theorem. The outer and inner edge of the single ring fit snugly around a square (third theorem), and so does the ring around the small circle in the right of the pictogram. Interestingly, I also discovered that the latter element seems to contain a new theorem, because the circle and the ring include an isosceles triangle (a triangle with two sides of the same length). Perhaps this does not seem to be so special at first glance; however, closer analysis shows that this can be considered as a special case of Hawkins's second theorem. Since the inner and outer edges of the ring are determined (because they have to fit around the included square), there exists only one way in which a central circle can fit inside an isosceles triangle, which for its own part fits inside the inner and outer edges of the ring. The top angle of such an isosceles triangle can be calculated (see Appendix B). It amounts to slightly less than 46 degrees. (See Figure 3-7.)

All these findings made one thing clear to me: This pictogram was definitely not created by the two young men who, according to a local newspaper, said they spontaneously decided to make a few circles for fun as they came along a field of

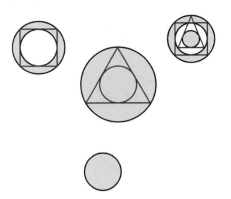

Figure 3-6. Hawkins's theorems applied to the pictogram's basic elements.

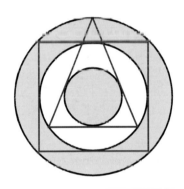

Figure 3-7. A derivative of Hawkins's second theorem? The central circle and the inner and outer edge of the surrounding ring include an isosceles triangle. Since the outer ring includes a square, this can only happen in one way, which defines the diameters of the ring and the circle, as well as the top angle of the triangle (slightly less than 46 degrees).

wheat. Making this unlikely is that despite its apparently simple design, the pictogram revealed an unsurpassed complexity and could never have been created without thorough preparation and highly accurate working methods. But what did it mean? Were all these structural findings a consequence of the way the circle creators worked? Was it a shadow of their technological limitations? Or was it an attempt by an entity that cannot get in direct contact with us and used a universal language to demonstrate its intelligence? Is this all a code that we are supposed to decipher? So far we only know one thing for sure: Coincidence can be ruled out.

The Melick Rings

ANOTHER GEOMETRICAL SYMBOL THAT OFTEN APPEARS DURING THE GEOmetric analysis of crop formations is the *pentagram,* or five-pointed star. Many crop circle formations can be enclosed by a pentagram around which a circle exactly touches the tramlines at both sides, as sketched in Figure 3-08.

This property is sometimes referred to as *fivefold geometry.* Quite a spectacular example, which combined three of Hawkins's theorems with pentagrams, appeared near the village of Melick, Holland, in the summer of 1997. The pictogram contained a small circle with three concentric rings around it (see Figure 3-9).

After an initial analysis I found that:

1. The center circle and the first ring enclosed an equilateral triangle (Hawkins II).

2. The first ring and the second ring enclosed a square (Hawkins III).

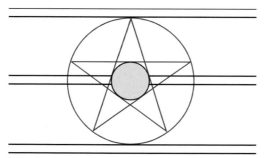

tramlines

Figure 3-8. Pentagram aligning a crop circle with respect to tramlines.

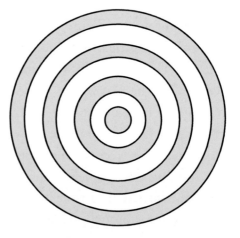

Figure 3-9. Melick, Holland, 1997.

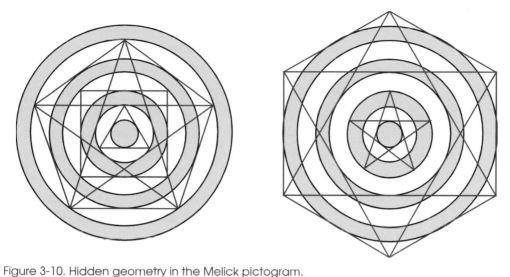

Figure 3-10. Hidden geometry in the Melick pictogram.

3. The second ring and the third ring enclosed a pentagon.

The total pictogram had a length of about 50 meters, and my measurements were accurate to about 10 centimeters. So these findings were already remarkable. However, after further analysis, I noticed that:

4. The pentagon contained a pentagram, which related the inner edge of the first ring to the inner edge of the third ring. (See Figure 3-10, left.)

This last finding complicated the design considerably. In order to fulfill all requirements 1 through 4, it is not sufficient that each ring around the center circle have the correct diameter with respect to the nearest enclosed ring (necessary for properties 1, 2, and 3). Explicit requirements must also be fulfilled for the *width* of the rings (note that the inner ring is indeed relatively thick). In order to determine these widths, one has to solve a set of equations with several variables, a mathematical problem that few people know how to approach. Moreover, it is a drastic complication in the design, requiring high accuracy during the creation of the pictogram.

But the discoveries were not over yet. It took me another two years or so, when one day I reconsidered the diagram as I had analyzed it and realized that there were still many different ways in which three rings around a central circle could fulfill the four properties that I had discovered in this example. Experiences with other, more complicated diagrams made me a little suspicious. I got the strong feeling that more geometric relationships had to be hidden in the rings, so as to define the exact diameters of *all* rings, both at the inner and the outer edges. And in fact, after a while I discovered another pentagram connecting the central circle with the outer edge of the first ring (see Figure 3-10, right). Moreover, and this was another astonishing finding: The last missing link in my analysis, needed to completely define the dimensions of all rings, was given by a *hexagon* around the third ring, which added itself to the sequence of the triangle, square, and pentagon. It meant that three-, four-, five- and sixfold geometry, exactly in that order, were hidden between the circle and its three successive rings. The hexagon around the third ring could be used to define a hexagram (six-pointed star) containing another, smaller hexagon in its center, which exactly enclosed the inner edge of the second ring (see Figure 3-10, right).

In order to make sure that my findings were not the effect of flaws in the geometrical construction, I compared all measured diameters with the theoretical values that would be required to obtain all these matches of a triangle, a square, a pentagon, two pentagrams, a hexagon, and a hexagram. The results can be seen in the table of Figure 3-11 (the actual analysis is described in Appendix C). The margins in the measured values result from the estimated measurement accuracy of 10 cm. It is seen that, within this accuracy, all six theoretic values are in agreement with the measurements. After making an estimate for the chance that this was accidental, I came up with a probability of one in forty-six million (1 in 46,000,000, which is roughly the chance of tossing a coin twenty-five times in a row to tails).

I concluded that the inner and outer diameters of all three rings had been carefully chosen so that each of them fulfilled one of the several well-known geometrical theorems. The diameters of all three rings were completely defined by the inner circle's diameter only. Figure 3-12 shows how all the different ring elements are geometrically related to each other.

	required proportions:	measured
Triangle	½=0.50	0.48±0.07
Square	½√2 ≈ 0.71	0.70±0.04
Pentagon	$\cos(\pi/5) \approx 0.81$	0.79±0.02
Small pentagram	$\dfrac{\tan(\pi/10)}{\tan(\pi/10)+\tan(\pi/5)} \approx 0.31$	0.30±0.04
Large pentagram	Idem, ≈ 0.31	0.29±0.02
Hexagram	$\dfrac{1}{3}\sqrt{3} \approx 0.57$	0.57±0.02

Figure 3-11. The Melick Rings, comparison of calculated and measured proportions.

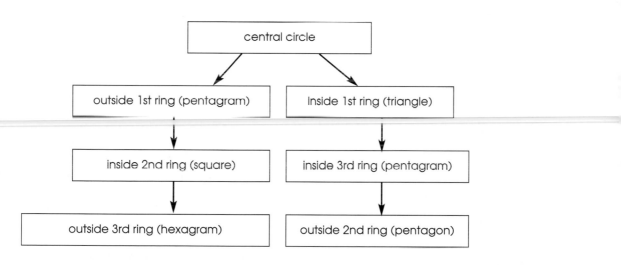

Figure 3-12. The Melick Rings. Design diagram, showing how all rings are determined, through geometrical relationships, by the diameter of the central circle only.

Construction Lines

As a follow-up to Hawkins's work, the Dutch crop circle researcher Bert Janssen performed excellent and much revealing work in crop circle geometry. A thorough description of Janssen's work would be beyond the scope of this book. However, I will describe in some detail the procedures of a geometrical analysis performed on a more complicated pictogram and will explain some of Janssen's most revealing findings. As an example, we will take the magnificent crop circle that appeared near the village of Alton Barnes, England, on July 9, 1998. I visited this formation the day after it had appeared and walked around in it for an hour, but even viewing it from a nearby hill, which was the highest point in the vicinity, it was impos-

Figure 3-13. Alton Barnes, England, July 9th, 1998. Photograph: Steve Alexander.

sible to understand the exact shape of its wiggly boundary. Only the day after, when I purchased an aerial photograph from crop circle photographer Steve Alexander (Figure 3-13), could the magnificent symmetry of the formation be appreciated.

As can be understood from this photograph, it is not at all a straightforward process to obtain a scaled copy of the formation's boundary on a drawing board by performing field measurements. A more efficient approach, in fact, is to take an aerial photograph and use a computer to trace the boundary of flattened crop. The result can be seen in Figure 3-14.

At this point the first complication arises. Before we can perform an analysis on the figure that we obtained, we have to correct for the perspective distortion, which results from the fact that the aerial photograph was not taken from straight above the center of the formation. Fortunately, some commercial computer programs, designed for the creation and manipulation of digital images, contain functionality that allows adding or changing the visual perspective of any chosen object. This is usually done by repositioning four points on a surrounding border, while the procedure basically looks like changing the view on a rectangular field seen from the air (see Figure 3-15). This procedure was performed on the boundary trace of the Alton Barnes formation.

In order to assure accuracy, we made use of the fact that the formation was roughly circular, with sevenfold symmetry. While correcting for the perspective, we therefore tried to align the boundary with fourteen (two times seven) equally

Figure 3-14. Boundary trace of Alton Barnes formation.

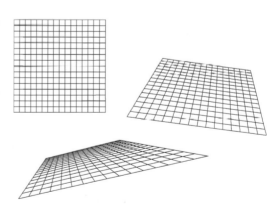

Figure 3-15. Changing visual perspective with a computer.

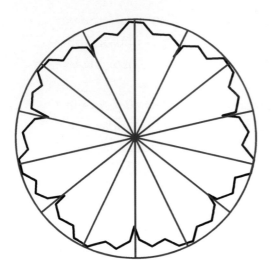

Figure 3-16. Alton Barnes crop circle, after perspective correction.

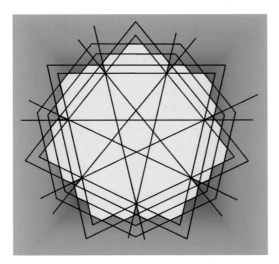

Figure 3-17. Geometrical construction lines for Alton Barnes formation.

sized circular segments. The result can be seen in Figure 3-16.

The next step consists of a combination of patience, mathematical insight, and gut feeling. Bert Janssen showed that the boundary could be constructed from a combination of concentric heptagons and sevenfold star shapes (heptagrams), as shown in Figure 3-17.[4] By carefully following specific parts of the guidelines, the Alton Barnes pictogram can be revealed. Please take a close look at the diagram, including all the guidelines, and appreciate the awesome complexity of this apparently simple shape.

The most fascinating part, however, has not been discussed yet, and this is without doubt one of Janssen's most revealing findings. If you look carefully at the aerial photograph (Figure 3-13), you will see two thin, shiny rings, concentric to the imprint, toward the edge. Janssen discovered that these two circles are needed to scale the other construction lines to their correct proportions.[5] Interestingly, these construction lines were indeed found—as thin lines of flattened stems—under the flattened crop in the main area. They indicated that the geometrical analysis presented earlier was indeed used for the actual construction of the pictogram. Janssen found similar construction lines in several other formations, leading to similar conclusions. Some would suggest that these construction lines, hidden under the flattened crop, are highly suspicious, and could in fact be indications of a hoax. However, and this is the interesting part: The construction lines were only found in the area of flattened crop, but never outside the physical imprint, in the standing crop. Think about this carefully. The fact that construction lines are found inside the area of flattened crop clearly indicates that they were apparently necessary for the geometrical construction of the formation in the field. However, when reconstructing the diagrams on a sheet of paper, these construction lines need to extend far outside the boundary of the resulting geometric shape, corresponding to positions in the field far away from the flattened area, hence, in the standing crop. But unlike a pencil line on a piece of paper, a construction line made in the standing crop cannot be erased afterwards. Nevertheless, the external sections of the construction lines have never been found. According to Janssen, there was in fact not even the slightest trace of any human activity outside the flattened area, no footprints, no crushed stems, nothing. According to Janssen, this finding is highly curious.

Of course one can think of advanced methods, using accurate localization equipment, which would allow someone to accurately trace any boundary designed earlier, including the one presented here. However, with such methods, one would not need any construction lines whatsoever. But the internal sections of the construction lines were unmistakably there, not only in the Alton Barnes formation of 1998, but also in many other formations investigated by Janssen. These findings defy any human logic, and according to Janssen are the ultimate proofs that the formations under study were not man-made.

Node Length Increase

I N A SCIENTIFIC PAPER PUBLISHED IN 1994, BIOPHYSICIST WILLAM C. LEVENgood first published his findings about a crop circle–related anomaly, presenting itself as swollen nodes or *pulvini* in corn-type plants inside crop formations.[6] These nodes, which can be easily recognized as the little "knuckles" along the stems of the plants, act as a sort of ligament, allowing the plants to bend upward after they are put in a horizontal position. Levengood suggested that the swelling results from a heating effect (possibly caused by microwave radiation), which makes the liquid core of the plant cells swell by thermal expansion, similar to the mercury inside a thermometer. The visco-elastic properties of the cell walls would ensure that the nodes kept their expanded shape, even after they cooled off.[7] (This very same property is utilized, for example, during the construction of musical instruments. A heat source—steam, or a hot copper pipe—is used to heat up a straight piece of wood, which can then be bent in a curved shape, which it will keep even after the wood cools off again.) The origin of the allegedly involved microwave radiation was not identified, but Levengood suggested that it might be related to plasma energies, somehow created in the atmosphere.

The node-lengthening effect is very real and has been demonstrated literally thousands of times. Levengood even indicated a relationship between the actual node length and the distance from the sampled plants to the geometric centers of the formations, which he attributed to the electromagnetic character of the radiation source.[8]

Over the years, quite a few people have claimed that they witnessed the formation of a crop circle by a "radiant ball of light." For example, in the night of June 7, 1999, a young Dutchman noticed a small light in the sky, which looked like a bright star over the field behind his house.[9] Suddenly he noticed that the light was moving and actually seemed to be quite close. The color of the light was a very faint pink, almost white. Then, in just a few seconds, the light transformed into an elliptic shape, which appeared to hover in the air at a height of about three meters, while the faint light seemed to shine down on the field. The air around it was trembling as if it were hot. Then the light slowly faded and disappeared. He ran into the field, where he discovered a fresh circle of flattened crop, and he noticed that the crop, the soil, and the air felt physically warm.

Less than a week after this remarkable event, a second formation appeared at a stone's throw from the first one. This time, a short light flash above the field was seen, as if a photograph were taken. The light seemed to emerge from a single point, flashing down on the field, and was of a bright white, very slightly bluish color. Upon inspection, another circle was found, which also felt physically warm. (See Figure 3-18.)

I was immediately contacted about this event, and after consultation with Nancy Talbott of the American BLT research team, I decided to visit the place to perform an extensive sampling of both formations and perform some simple experiments on the collected material. The two circles, both nine meters

Figure 3-18. The crop circle, allegedly created by a "ball of light," according to a local eyewitness (Noord-Brabant, Holland, 1999).

in diameter, were sampled in twenty-seven positions, all circularly symmetric, with approximately twenty stems per sampling point (see sampling diagram, Figure 3-19). The objective was to investigate the average node length

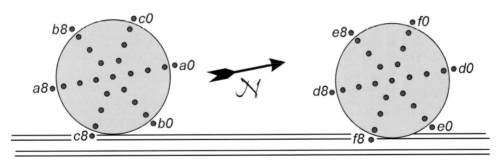

tramlines

Figure 3-19. Sampling diagram of the two Dutch crop circles. At each dot about 20–25 stems + seedheads were taken. Furthermore, nine control samples were taken throughout the field, at different locations, all far away from the circles.

for each sample and compare this value with control samples taken in the upright crop, far away from the imprints. My particular interest was to determine the variation of the average node length over the physical imprint of the two formations, so as to reveal any clues related to the symmetry of the energies involved in crop circle formation.

A total of more than 1,500 stems were collected, taped together, and labeled. After the samples had been thoroughly dried over a few months (taking care to hang them in such a way that they would not be eaten by mice), the measurements were made. (See Figure 3-20.)

Figure 3-20. Crop circle samples, wrapped and labeled.

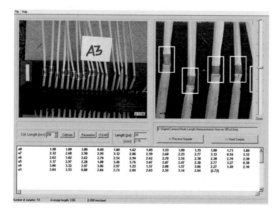

Figure 3-21. Optical node length measurements on a PC.

In order to accurately measure fifteen hundred nodes with a dimension of only a few millimeters, I wrote a computer program that would do the work for me. With this helpful tool, all I had to do was clamp each bunch of stems between iron pins and make a digital photograph (see Figure 3-21). The computer program then managed to measure the length of each node with an accuracy of a tenth of a millimeter. This all may seem somewhat compulsive, but I can guarantee you that measuring 1,500 labeled nodes with a caliper and writing down the measured values by hand would be unnecessarily tedious, and would fill many with despair. More importantly, if you lose your concentration halfway through your work (which is more than likely to occur), you run the risk of completely messing up the entire experiment. Finally, the fact that the measurements were done by a computer guaranteed the ultimate blind study, without any experimenter's bias.

The Node Length Results

THE GRAPH SHOWN IN FIGURE 3-22, WITH THE GREEN BARS, SHOWS THE results for the control measurements. The height of each bar represents the average length of the nodes in each of the nine bunches of stems that were taken out of the undisturbed, standing crop, far away from the circles. On the vertical axis it can be seen that each bar corresponds to a length of about two millimeters. This was indeed a normal length for the nodes at their particular state of maturity.

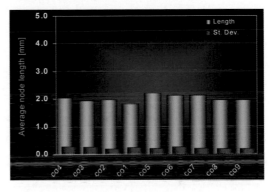

As you can see, not all bars are the same length. There is a slight variation over the different samples. This is a result of normal, biologic variations over the samples, because no two stems in a sample are exactly identical, and no two nodes have exactly the same length. From a collection of nodes one can derive a number, the so-called *standard deviation,* which tells us how much variation there is between the length of individual nodes in each sample. This value is indicated by the red bars in the graph. So the first green bar at the left, representing the control sample labeled CO4, indicates that the average length of all nodes in the sample amounted to slightly more than 2 mm, whereas the variations between the individual nodes in the sample were in the order of 0.3 mm. The exact measured values for the nineteen nodes at position CO4, in millimeters, are listed here:

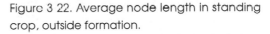
Figure 3-22. Average node length in standing crop, outside formation.

1.85	2.34	1.95	2.24	1.85
2.34	1.76	2.34	2.15	1.85
2.24	2.05	1.95	1.95	1.95
2.34	2.34	1.95	1.95	

The conclusion that can be reached from this graph is twofold: (1) The average node length in the undisturbed crop was around two millimeters, and (2) there was a slight variation of the average node length at different locations in the field (possibly an effect of wind, sunlight, local differences in the soil composition, or the amount of fertilizer), but these were within the standard deviation for each sample, and hence not significant.

Next we take a look at the node length inside the crop circle that was allegedly created by the faint, pink light source. Remember how the samples were taken: Sample a0 (20–25 stems) was taken at one edge; samples a1, a2, and a3 at equal distances toward the center; sample a4 at the center; a5, a6, and a7 at the opposite side of the center; and a8 at the opposite edge (see Figure 3-23). A first glance at the graph immediately shows that the average node length at some positions inside the crop circle is considerably more than the length of the controls. In the center, the average length amounts to 4.28 mm, more than twice the length of the control samples. There are known mechanisms that explain an increase in node length after a crop is flattened, such as gravitropism, which is the natural effect that makes a plant straighten up after it is pressed down. However, earlier studies indicated that this mechanism could not account for more than a ten to twenty percent node length increase in a period of a week.[10] In this particular case we found an increase of more than a factor of two, which is remarkable.

Even more striking is the fact that the lengths of the bars in the graph are perfectly symmetric with respect to the center bar (representing the center of the circle). This is an extraordinary, astonishing finding, for the following reason. Suppose that the crop circle was man-made by flattening the crop with the aid of a plank and a rope, as many always want us to believe. Apart from the fact that this could never explain the abnormally large increase in node length, one

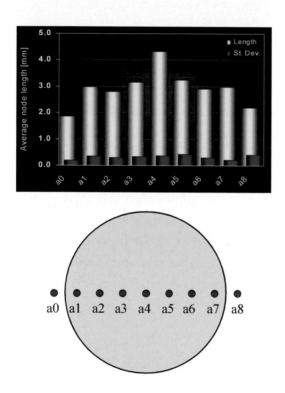

Figure 3-23. Average node length inside crop circle, from one edge (a0) along the center (a4) towards the opposite edge (a8).

should also consider the fact that after the crop is flattened, each stem in the crop circle experiences identical environmental conditions. After all, it is just crop flattened in a circular pattern. So each stem inside the circle experiences exactly the same temperature, the same amount of humidity, and the same amount of light. But how is it possible, then, that the growth of the stem nodes depends on the distance from the center of the circle? How does a plant close to the center know it has to make its nodes swell more than the plants at the edge do? How does a plant know that there is a circular imprint in the field, and where its own position in that circle is? The answer is simple: The plant does not know. So the symmetry in the node swelling must have another explanation.

At this point it is useful to consider the average node length along the other two cross sections through the circle. The corresponding graphs can be seen in Figure 3-24. The astronomically small chance that the symmetry in the previous graph was purely accidental is reduced further still by the

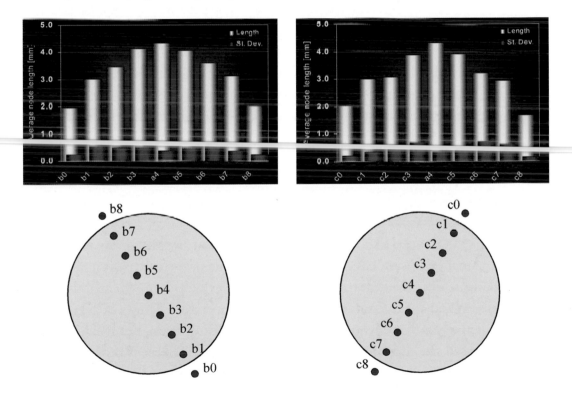

Figure 3-24. Average node length inside crop circle along the two other cross sections.

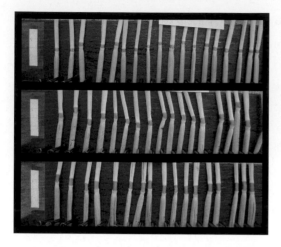

Figure 3-25. Node samples from the Noord-Brabant formation, clearly showing the drastic and structured increase in node length at positions a0 (top), a3 (middle) and a4 (bottom), corresponding to the edge of the circle, halfway to the center, and the center.

other two graphs, which contain exactly the same symmetry we found earlier. I cannot emphasize it enough: This is a highly interesting finding. Thanks to the large number of samples, the statistical relevance is 100 percent, and the measurements show clearly that the average node swelling over the formation has the same symmetry as the imprint in the field itself: circular. This is a strong indication that whatever created the circle also caused the node swelling at the same time. The statement by the eyewitness about an intense heat inside the formation, shortly after it was created, is another indication for what caused the node swelling: heat and thermal expansion of the water-filled nodes. Earlier I had performed alternative analyses on results published by Levengood, which had made me suspect that node lengthening may indeed be caused by the curious "balls of light." The large amount of data available from this particular study allowed a reasonable justification of this hypothesis. The results will be presented in the next section. (See Figure 3-25.)

BOL Analysis

As suggested by Levengood, node length increase may be a thermal expansion effect. The liquid contents of the cells heat up, while at the same time the heat makes the cell walls flexible. Consequently, the plant cells expand as a reaction to the increasing temperature. However, as explained earlier, when the cells cool off, they will not shrink again, but will keep their increased size. If we assume that the node length increase is proportional to the temperature increase (which is a reasonable assumption, as this is how a thermometer measures temperature), the nodes may actually be used as if they were tiny memory thermometers. In other words, the node lengths that were determined at various locations may be used as indicators for local temperature at the time the crop circle was created.

Next we assume that the eyewitness has indeed made an accurate observation, and that the heat was induced by the ball of light while it was hanging above the field. Mind you, many other people say they have seen similar things happen, and the "balls of light" have actually been observed so often that they have their own acronym: BOLs. Determining the heat distribution of a spherical source of electromagnetic radiation ("light") is straightforward. Neglecting the absorption in the air (which is reasonable in this case), we may use the property that the intensity of an electromagnetic point source decreases proportionally to distance squared. In other words: Two times further away makes the radiation four times less, three times further away makes it nine times less, and so on. If we assume that the BOL was at a height h above the field, the distance between the BOL and a point at distance d from the center of the circle amounts to

$$r = \sqrt{h^2 + d^2}$$

as pointed out a long time ago by the Greek mathematician Pythagoras.

At this point, we have created a mathematical model, which can be used to predict the temperature distribution on ground level, throughout the circle. (See Figure 3-26.) The next thing we will do is to try to match our measurements shown in the previous paragraph with this model. This can be done in many ways, but we will employ a method known as linear regression analysis. This method represents the measurements as points on a graph, in such a way that a good fit to the mathematical model is indicated when the points appear in a straight line. The result of such an analysis can be seen in Figure 3-27. The verti-

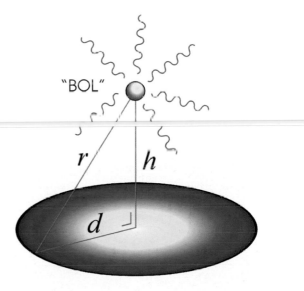

Figure 3-26. "Ball of light" (BOL) at a height h above a crop circle with radius d. The radiation intensity emitted by the BOL will be highest at the center of the crop circle and decrease towards its edge.

cal axis represents the measured node length increase (as compared with the control samples); the horizontal axis represents the distance between the BOL (set at a height of 4.1 meters) and the positions where the samples were taken. We see that the measurements, indicated by the red dots, are indeed positioned along a straight line. This confirms that the heat distribution on the ground was identical to the temperature that would have been induced by a small electromagnetic source, in this case at a position of 4.1 meters above the field. The match of our measurements to the model can be expressed by a number, which is known as the Pearson or correlation coefficient. The closer this number is to 1, the better the fit. The Pearson coefficient in this particular case amounts to 0.988, indicating a near-perfect fit.

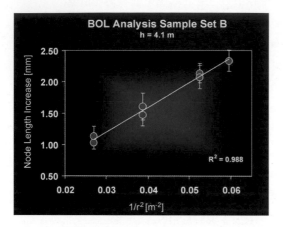

Figure 3-27. Linear regression analysis of the node length along trace b, assuming heating by a point source at a height of 4.1 m. The measurement (red dots) appear on a straight line, which indicates that the measured node lengths correspond perfectly to the radiation intensity emitted by a small spherical electromagnetic source.

The consequences of this finding are most intriguing. It all started with an eyewitness who declared that he saw a crop circle appear underneath a small, anomalous light source floating in the air above the field. Of course such a statement is extremely peculiar and would make anyone suspicious. Perhaps this person was just looking at the moon disappearing behind a cloud? Perhaps he was drunk? Perhaps he invented it all, just for fun? There are dozens of trivial explanations, which are much easier to believe than a story about an unidentified light source creating a crop circle. Nevertheless, the results shown here prove that there was, in fact, physical evidence left in the field,

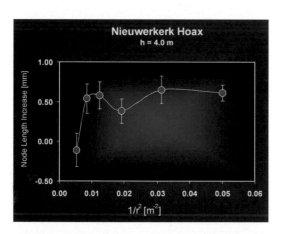

Figure 3-27b. Identical analysis, performed on a man-made hoax.

supporting the eyewitness account beyond any reasonable doubt.

A similar analysis was also performed on node length measurements published by Levengood, which were obtained from three different crop formations in the U.S. and England.[11] The results were identical: The linear regression coefficients all had values close to unity, indicating evidence for an electromagnetic point source that caused the node-swelling effect. Interestingly, the same analysis performed on an elaborate man-made formation that I had investigated earlier (Dreischor, Holland, 1997) revealed a very bad linear regression fit, as would be expected. I compiled these findings in an article, which I submitted to a peer-reviewed journal on plant physiology and biophysics, Physiologia Plantarum. ("Peer-reviewed" journals have one or more experts review each submitted contribution in order to check the contents of the article for erroneous methods, inconsistencies, preliminary conclusions, and so on. If these are found, the article is not accepted for publication.) Although it took the board of referees almost six months, eventually the article was approved and published.[12]

This publication has an important consequence. It means that the hypothesis that "balls of light" are directly involved in the creation of (at least some of the) crop formations is no longer a hypothesis, but a scientifically proven and accepted fact. Moreover, it will remain such a fact until someone comes forward with an alternative explanation for the circularly symmetric node lengthening, or proofs that the analysis was erroneous. However, such a proof will not be an article in some daily newspaper or on the Internet. The discussions about node-lengthening effects in crop circles have clearly outgrown the level of the tabloids and entered the era of scientific communication by means of scientific literature. Consequently, the only comment that can be taken seriously at this point will have to be another publication in a peer-reviewed scientific journal.

Finally, it is important to acknowledge that all these findings presented here and in the Physiologia Plantarum article support the earlier conclusions reached by Levengood, indicating the electromagnetic character of the "circle energies." Moreover, they rigorously pull the apparently controversial video recordings and photographs of BOLs out of the twilight zone. It seems as if science has taken another step forward toward unraveling the crop circle mysteries.

Germination Tests

THE REMARKABLE FINDINGS DESCRIBED IN THE PREVIOUS PARAGRAPH OBVIously tempted me to perform a simple germination test as well. For each sample, seeds were taken out of ten different seedheads, resulting in ten seeds per sample. In order to approach an identical environment for each sample during germination, all seeds were put together in small garden frames, with each bucket containing the same amount of potting compost, while every two days identical quantities of water were given to all samples. The garden frame was put in front of a large window so all seedlings would receive the same amount of light. After only a few days, tremendous differences in development could be seen.

Skeptics have suggested that these effects are the mere result of physical damage to the seeds caused by the mechanical flattening process and foot stomping. However, one of the remarkable findings about crop circles is that the plants remain completely undamaged, without the slightest trace of mechanical forces. Nevertheless, before the seeds were pulled out, all seedheads were carefully checked for mechanical damage, which was not found in any of them. Also, no obvious visual differences between the individual seeds or between the seeds of different samples were observed. Another argument that negates the hypothesis that germination differences are just the effect of mechanical damage can be seen from the photograph in Figure 3-28. The seedlings in the third column from the left, for example, are small compared to most of the other samples. However, the length difference between individual seedlings in one sample is much less than the length differences between different samples. In other words, *all* the seedlings in one sample show the same anomalous germination behavior, not just a few. Each bucket contained ten seeds, with each seed taken from a different plant, and

Figure 3-28. Germination test, showing the situation after a week. Note the differences in germination speed!

there is no possibility that mechanical damage would produce such a controlled disturbance of the seed germination process.

After two weeks, all seedlings were carefully removed from their containers, rinsed with water, and measured. The results can be seen in Figure 3-29. The graph at the top left shows the average seedling length of the controls. The green bars indicate an average length of about 140 mm, with a moderate spread (standard deviation) in each sample, indicated as before by the red bars. The length variation of the green bars is about the same as the lengths of the red bars, indicating that these differences are just natural variations in germination speed. The situation is quite different for the crop circle seedlings. As can be seen immediately in the other three graphs, seeds taken at different positions in the crop circle revealed tremendous differences in seedling development. In several locations, germination speed was reduced up to a factor of four or so. At the same time, however, the seedlings in each sample all had more or less the same length. This can again be seen

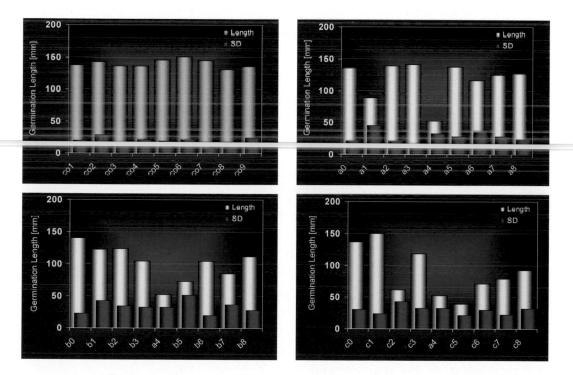

Figure 3-29. Germination test results, showing average seedling length after two weeks for controls (top left) and crop circle samples.

from the red bars, which show the spread in length between the individual seedlings in one bucket, which is small.

At this point it must be mentioned once again that a decrease in germination speed has been reported many times by the BLT research team. Moreover, the large amount of samples considered here indicate clearly that the germination anomalies are less structured than the node length increase. This can be seen when one compares the smooth and symmetric node length graphs shown earlier with the apparent random-length bars in the germination graphs. It shows that germination disturbance is a highly nonlinear process, unlike node length increase, which seems more structured. Nevertheless, it is interesting to note from the germination graphs that in the center of the circle (where the node length increase was high), the average seedling length tends to be more reduced than at the edges. This would be an indication that the radiation emitted by the BOL not only heats up the plants, but also damages the seeds in the same process.

In order to verify this hypothesis, one can produce a graph that shows the relationship between average node length and average seedling length of all samples taken from the crop circle. This is shown in Figure 3-30. Although the graph does not indicate a strong correlation, the yellow regression line (indicating the tendency of the points) does indicate that seedling length decreases with node length, presumably as a result of higher electromagnetic radiation levels. Finally, it must be mentioned that this observation is in agreement with earlier findings by Levengood. When crop circles appear early in the season, as in this case, germination speeds tend to reduce. Crop circles appearing in mature crop, close to harvest, tend to reveal the opposite effect: increased germination speed in comparison with controls.

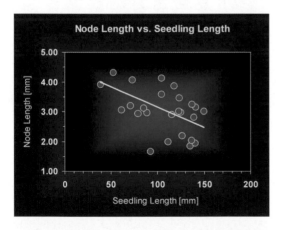

Figure 3-30. Relationship between node length and seedling length. The graph shows that longer nodes tend to be related to shorter seedling lengths.

Light Orb Photography

IT WILL BE CLEAR FROM PREVIOUS SECTIONS OF THIS BOOK THAT THE CURI-
ous light balls or BOLs seem to form a very real phenomenon. In fact, ever
since crop circles have appeared, anomalous light effects have been reported
by many eyewitnesses. The vast number of accounts, an abundant amount
of photographic and in particular video material, and the physical analysis presented in the previous paragraphs prove the existence of the BOLs, sometimes simply referred to as *light orbs* or—for reasons unclear to me—*plasma
balls*. At the same time, with the increasing awareness of these anomalous
light phenomena, many "cerealogists" have published a wealth of photo-

graphs of these "plasma balls" in newspapers, books, magazines, and of course
on the Internet (see, for example, Figure
3-31). Some of this material comes with
reports of interesting characteristics:

Figure 3-31. Crop circle with "plasma balls."

• The plasma balls can be photographed
with ordinary equipment, but seem to
appear only on photographs taken in
the dark, with a flash.

• They are often spherical, with intricate
details in intensity, and often with a
clear rim around them.

• When different researchers photograph
these plasma balls, each seems to record
different shapes (circular, hexagonal,
diamond-shaped, square, etc.).

Zooming in to one of these spheres,
one recognizes the intricate details and
the rim (see Figure 3-32). Needless to say,
the plasma balls also appear on the photographic negative and even on pictures

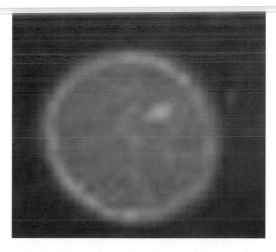

Figure 3-32. "Plasma Ball," close up.

taken with a digital camera, excluding artifacts from chemical processing. The examples shown here, however, and without any doubt the majority of "plasma balls" photographed and published by others, are a nice example of "what you seek is what you get." When a flash photograph is taken in the pitch dark, the camera will produce the brightest flash the hardware permits, as can usually be seen on the overilluminated foreground. Due to the limited range of the flash, however, large parts of the photograph will nevertheless remain dark. Consequently, any tiny little speck of dust, any tiny raindrop or mist particle, or anything similar floating in the air within reach of the camera flash will produce a relatively bright reflection. Particles far away from the camera flash will not be captured; however, those at shorter distances will appear as large smears of light (because they will be out of focus), the shape of which will depend on their exact distance and the specific optical system of the camera. They might take the shape of the camera's diaphragm (circular, hexagonal, diamond-shaped, square), although usually circular spots will be seen. The curious nomenclature "plasma ball" should therefore be replaced by *UFO* instead, in this case meaning *unfocused object*. In fact, most of these so-called anomalies can be easily explained.

By no means do I intend to reject all anomalous light phenomena related to crop circles, as will be clear to you from my previous statements. However, an investigation into the origin of this matter takes much more than a simple photo camera and a flash. The least one should do is:

- Use a digital, stereoscopic camera (so that processing flaws can be eliminated, while this would allow measurement of the distance and size of the light objects).

- Work without a flash first (photographing delicate light effects with a flash is not the first thing you do and actually clashes with common sense).

Ordinary, single-shot photographs can never be conclusive. This is illustrated in Figure 3-33 by a flash photograph of my three-year-old daughter on New Year's Eve. The ball artifacts are induced by extremely small smoke particles caused by the fireworks. I could see these artifacts right after I took the pictures, thanks to the digital camera I was using. Intrigued, I made many more photographs and noted how the artifacts disappeared as soon

THE SCIENTIFIC PERSPECTIVES

as the smoke had cleared away.

The photograph in Figure 3-34 was taken at night, with a flash, during a light snowfall. It is clearly seen that the small snowflakes, as they approach the camera, get out of focus and transform into spherical "plasma balls," including the delicate details (possibly a light interference effect) and the rim.

The lesson we learn from this is that we should never make too big a conclusion during the study of uncommon phenomena. We should always take care not to become overenthusiastic and fool ourselves. It is my sincere opinion that many conclusions reached by others are premature. Of course this is not a particularly world-shattering finding, but there is a bad side effect. Ill-founded articles and premature or inaccurate conclusions made by those with apparently no

Figure 3-33. Ball artifacts induced by camera flash and smoke particles.

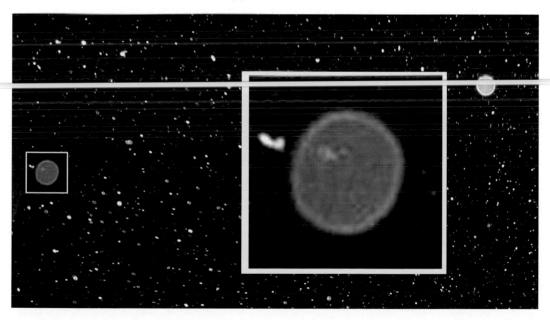

Figure 3-34. Ball artifacts induced by camera flash and small snowflakes. Insert: close up. Note the resemblance with the alleged "plasma ball" in Figure 3-32.

profound knowledge of the equipment they use (in this case optical lens systems) cast a dark shadow on the crop circle phenomenon in general, which is already under the fire of (often undeserved) skepticism. I am convinced that there is a genuine and highly interesting mechanism behind a considerable part of the crop circle phenomenon, including incomprehensible light effects, while serious researchers have collected enough evidence to convince anyone with a reasonable amount of common sense. Getting this message out, however, is extremely difficult, and poorly researched, premature articles will seriously reduce the chance that crop circles will one day get the public attention they deserve.

More Research

MUCH MORE CROP CIRCLE-RELATED RESEARCH, AT VARIOUS LEVELS, HAS been performed by a number of investigators. For nonscientists, however, it is not always easy to judge the value of this work. I find that, in many cases, insufficient effort is put into the exclusion of trivial explanations and in an accurate description of the methods, procedures, and equipment that were used. This is a crucial part of any scientific experiment, but most of the time not enough attention is paid to it. Unfortunately, incomplete logging makes any experiment worthless and inconclusive. In addition, the use of impressive, advanced equipment does not guarantee proof. In fact, the more advanced the equipment, the higher the skills and knowledge of the operator must be. For example, experiments with ultrasensitive magnetic field measuring equipment will always show deviations of the earth-magnetic field in any crop circle. However, only an advanced measuring protocol, including solid statistics, will make a serious conclusion possible (that may well indicate a piece of rock with high iron content buried somewhere in the field). Measurements with high-sensitivity, broadband radio receivers are even more difficult to interpret, since our atmosphere teems with all kinds of radio waves, most created by humans, but even some created by nature. Your equipment will always indicate something, but how can you be sure of the cause? I am not saying it is impossible, but it takes more than a healthy dose of enthusiasm and a home-made device to reach scientifically valid conclusions. In my opinion, serious crop circle research has been very limited so far. The reason is simple: Research costs money and will never take place without solid funding. And as long as the public is not aware of their true nature, crop circles will never get the attention needed to raise funds.

Fortunately, some scientists seem to find a way of producing interesting and robust results. For example, the article published on the Internet by Marshall Dudley and Michael Chorost presents a substantial report about the discovery of thirteen short-lived radionuclides (radioactive isotopes) in soil samples taken from an English crop circle, including tellurium-119m, lead-203, and rhodium-102, with a natural lifetime of days only.[13] The isotopes were found in two soil samples taken within the crop circle and were absent in a control sample taken ten meters outside the formation. The presence of these particular short-lived radionuclides is surprising, since they must be synthesized in particle accelerators or experimental nuclear reactors, which makes them very difficult and expensive to obtain. According to the authors, a possible explanation for the simultaneous presence of all these radionuclides could be activation of naturally occurring elements with deuterium (heavy hydrogen) nuclei. Deuterium, an isotope of hydrogen, is not rare; it exists freely in nature and without doubt also in crop circles. However, deuterium nuclei would only be able to create the reported isotopes if they were in the highly energetic state of one mega-electronvolt (in very simple terms, the energy of 9,091 electric sockets in a row). Where exactly such highly energetic deuterium nuclei could have come from remains a big question.

The BLT Team

ANOTHER GROUP THAT PERFORMS EXCELLENT WORK IS THE BLT TEAM, consisting of the American researchers William C. Levengood, John Burke, and Nancy P. Talbott. Thousands of plant samples from crop circles around the world have been scientifically tested by Dr. Levengood, a semi-retired scientist with a seed consulting business in Michigan, who has published over 50 papers in the scientific literature (including three on the crop circle phenomenon.)[14]

The BLT team performs many different types of laboratory tests. One of the things that was discovered in the early days was a markedly reduced seed head size in comparison with controls when a formation formed in immature crop. Sometimes, a few weeks after a crop circle had appeared, the seed heads in the physical imprint would have no seeds inside them whatsoever. Occasionally, if seeds were present, they were severely stunted, smaller, and lighter. They produced struggling seedlings with severely reduced growth—if they survived the laboratory experiments at all. Levengood also discovered enlarged cell wall pits in bract tissue. (Bract tissue is a very thin membrane surrounding the seed heads; cell wall pits are small holes in the cell walls used for ion transportation.) Levengood assumes that the cell wall pits enlarge because heat hits the plants when the circles are created. But the most significant finding that the BLT team has come up with results from the seed germination trials. As mentioned earlier, when a formation is formed in immature crop, usually the seedlings do not develop at all, or at a largely reduced rate. However, if a crop formation occurs in mature crop, seedlings may grow at up to *five times* the normal rate. These trials have been done thousands of times. The BLT team states that their findings are consistent with the hypothesis that highly energetic, ionized plasma vortex systems are involved in the creation of crop circles and that changes to our upper atmosphere (loss of ozone?) might be indicated. BLT Research has also concluded that human interference is definitely not the causative factor in most crop formations, as stated, for example, in the 1999 *Physiologia Plantarum* article:

> Not one of these clearly anomalous plant alterations had been mentioned—much less explained—by the proponents of the vandal theory, nor can they be accounted for by the supposed methods employed to create crop formations through claims made by the self-described vandals.[15]

Notes

1. Pat Delgado and Colin Andrews, *Circular Evidence* (London: Bloomsbury Press, 1989).

2. Analysis reperformed by the author, from G. S. Hawkins, "The Diatonic Ratios in Crop Circles," *Circles Phenomenon Research International Newsletter* 5, no. 2 (1997): 2.

3. G. S. Hawkins, "Crop Circles: Theorems in Wheat Fields," *Science News* 150, no. 12 (October 1996): 239.

4. www.cropcircleconnector.com/Bert/bert98a4.html.

5. See note 4 above.

6. W. C. Levengood, "Anatomical Anomalies in Crop Formation Plants," *Physiologia Plantarum* 92 (1994): 356–363.

7. J. K. E. Ortega, "Governing Equations for Plant Cell Growth," *Physiologia Plantarum* 79 (1990): 116–121.

8. W. C. Levengood and N. P. Talbott, "Dispersion of Energies in Worldwide Crop Formations," *Physiologia Plantarum* 105 (1999): 615–624.

9. A more extensive account has been published by Nancy Talbott on the Internet at www.cropcircleconnector.com/archives/inter99/Hoeven 99a.html, and in Linda Moulton Howe's book, *Mysterious Lights and Crop Circles,* Paper Chase Press, 2001.

10. Studies performed by Burke, Levengood, and Talbott (BLT Research). See lab reports #27 (1994) and #86 (1997).

11. See note 8 above.

12. E. H. Haselhoff, "Dispersion of Energies in Worldwide Crop Formations" (Opinions and Comments), *Physiologia Plantarum* 111, vol. 1 (2000): 124.

13. www.zetatalk.com/theword/twordo2e.htm.

14. W. C. Levengood and John A. Burke, "Semi-Molten Meteoric Iron Associated with a Crop Formation," *Journal of Scientific Exploration* 9, no. 2 (1995): 191–199. Also see notes 6 and 8 above.

15. See note 8 above.

Stonehenge, England, 1996. This world famous formation, consisting of 151 circles, had a width of 115 meters and appeared during daytime, within a period of 45 minutes.

Photograph © Dr. Andrew King.

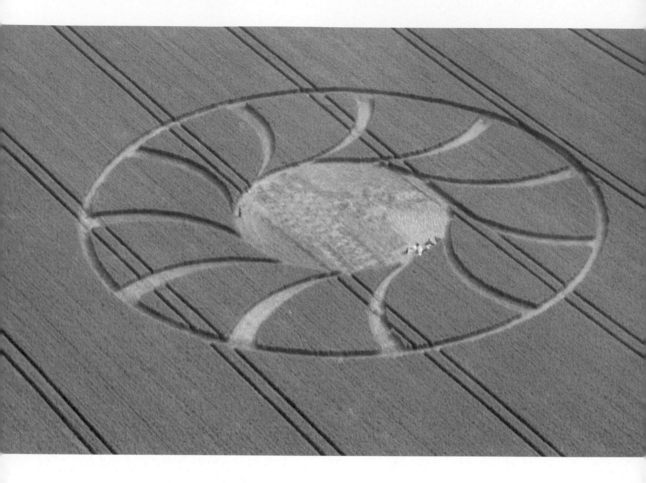

Beckhampton, England, 2000.
Photograph © Bert Janssen.

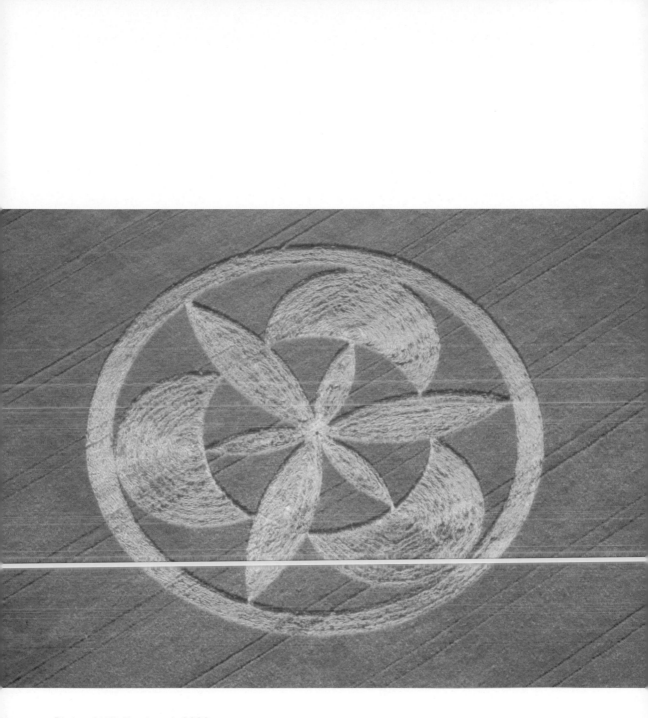

Picked Hill, England, 2000.
Photograph © Janet Ossebaard.

Windmill Hill, England, 1999.
Photograph © Dr. Andrew King.

East Kennett, England, 2000.
Photograph © Bert Janssen.

Stadskanaal, Holland, 2000.

Photograph © Eltjo Haselhoff.

Stadskanaal, Holland, 2000. This photograph was made from the ground with the camera mounted on a long pole, and shows the center part of the pictogram.

Photograph © Eltjo Haselhoff.

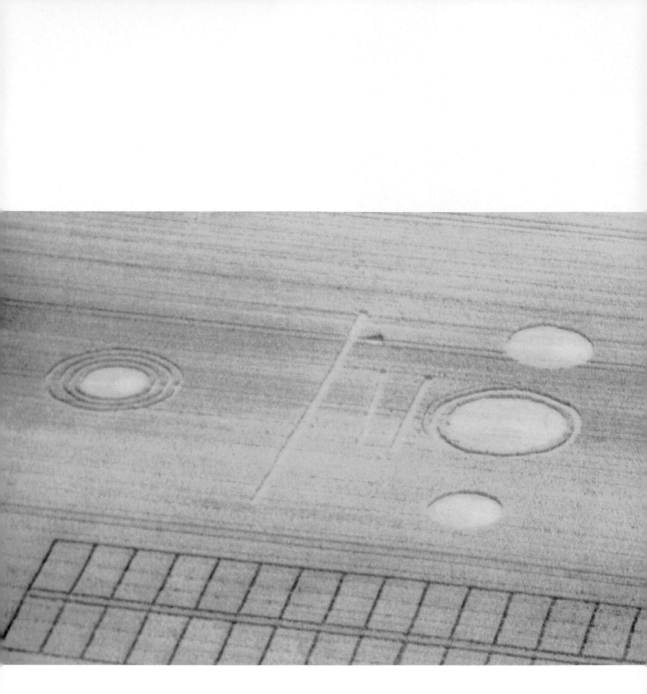

Zuid-Limburg, Holland, 1996. This magnificent formation was spotted from an airplane, but its exact location is unknown and the formation has never been reported. Interestingly, it was a near-perfect copy of a British formation that appeared six years earlier in Bratton Castle, on July 25, 1990.
Photograph © Arjan Dekker.

Chapter 4

The Psychic Perspectives

In the previous chapters, we have restricted ourselves to a factual consideration of the crop circle phenomenon. And even though many of the discussed observations are not yet understood, the observations themselves are straightforward and reproducible. Crop circles continue to appear throughout the year, all over the world, and some probably close to your own home. This means that anyone who doubts my words can perform his or her own analyses and experiments, according to scientific guidelines, and draw his or her own conclusions. But of course there are various ways of approaching the crop circle phenomenon. In fact, most of those who are involved treat the phenomenon in a nonscientific, spiritual, or psychic way. In the eyes of many, and particularly in the eyes of scientists, this approach has little or no value for the understanding of the underlying mechanisms. Nevertheless, many crop circle enthusiasts swear by the paranormal approach and claim that crop circles can only be understood by personal, emotional experience and not by rationality. Consequently, a book about crop circles would not be complete without paying some attention to this side of the story as well. Rather than compiling a comprehensive survey of the different schools of thought (which would in fact be a rather rational approach), I will simply relate some of the most startling "psychic" communications I have had over the years and add my personal opinion every now and then. Many of these stories may sound implausible, but then again, so was the account of an anomalous ball of light that allegedly created a crop circle, as discussed in the previous chapter. Yet in this case hard physical evidence was discovered, firmly corroborating the story. Apparently, it never hurts to listen.

Earth Forces

A COUPLE OF YEARS AGO I BECAME ACQUAINTED WITH AN ENGLISHMAN, Michael Newark, who shared his extraordinary view on the crop circle phenomenon with me. He believes crop circles are the result of a combined action of different natural earth forces. Some formations he believes are made by the unknown Circlemakers, while others are created by nature spirits: male or female devas. He says he can actually feel the "earth energies" when he is inside a crop formation, but also when he holds little objects taken from the formation (pebbles, ears, soil) in his hands.[1] (Interestingly, through the years I have met many people who claim to experience the same thing.) Michael experiences the symbols of the crop formations in a very special way. He feels that the "power" of the pictograms is integrated into the symbols to such an extent that just a simple diagram allows him to get in mental contact with the Circlemakers. "The presence of the natural power is retained in a copy of the diagram," according to Michael. "Don't ask me how. I know when I sometimes work with crop circles before bed, the open books and drawings I leave on my table creak and rustle in the dark. This does not happen when I leave the pictures or photos covered. I always have the feeling someone is looking through them in the dark."

Although Michael is not an overreligious person, he does see the crop circles as a sign of God.

> People are losing faith with God because he does not seem to be around us anymore, with so many bad things happening around the planet. The bad things we can see and feel, but God's work comes to us in a more subtle way. His approach is pictures in the fields, opening people's eyes and minds to his continuing existence and presence. God does not strike people down for sinning anymore, he wins the hearts and minds of the people in other ways, and I think crop circles are just one way he does this. We all must learn to live together, and know the path to heaven we will some day walk has many other paths which join it. And from these other paths all people of the world walk the last mile as friends. I think it is God's will we should see all men as brothers in this life, and all men equal.

Michael is convinced that the natural earth forces involved in the creation of crop circles are at least as old as humankind itself and closely related to the mystic properties attributed to holy ancient sites like Stonehenge, the Rollright Stones of Oxfordshire, Mekka, and Medina. He is also convinced that these forces were much better understood by our prehistoric ancestors than by ourselves. "Now is a good time to be alive," he said to me, "to experience crop circles and walk in the formations. Each genuine crop circle is right out of God's garden. Ancient men knew this, and we are just learning it as well. I think the message each crop circle brings is simple: *God is alive and well,* whatever religion you follow."

Aliens

IN THE YEAR 1996, WHEN THE SOUTH OF HOLLAND WAS LITERALLY STUDDED with crop circles, I got acquainted with Bob Snackers. I soon learned that he was considered a local expert in the field of "extraterrestrial activities on earth," not least because of personal experience. Over a few years he had had frequent contacts with an entity, which in his firm belief was extraterrestrial, and with which he communicated telepathically. Bob is one of the many people who claims to carry an "implant" in his body (in his case inside his head), which has been inserted by extraterrestrial beings, perhaps in order to allow or facilitate telepathic communication. "The implants need to be refreshed regularly," according to Bob,

> and the last time I was refreshed was in the seventies. It happened in my sleep. While I was asleep, I suddenly heard these high-pitched, whispering voices. I wondered what it could be, and tried to wake up, but I couldn't. Then, all of a sudden, it felt as if a little bug crawled in the inside of my head, and I thought, what on earth is that? Nevertheless, after a few days I had forgotten all about the incident, until a few weeks later I watched a television documentary on TV. It contained an interview with a woman somewhere in Africa; she was supposed to be crazy or schizophrenic or something. She told about exactly the same experience, about a little bug crawling to the inside of her head. And then I thought, oh my God, because I could not believe what I heard.

All over the world many people believe they have been visited or kidnapped by extraterrestrial beings, and many of them remember the surgical procedures during which "implants" were inserted in their bodies. In some cases these implants were surgically removed, resulting in a curious collection of small, more or less unusual objects. In a number of cases, after removal of the implants, the alleged visits by the extraterrestrials to the owner of the implant suddenly stopped. This fact, of course, supported the hypothesis that the implants are somehow used to track people down.

"And I am not the only one with an implant," said Bob. "There are many more people like myself, and also women, acting as surrogate mothers for the extraterrestrials."

Bob claims these extraterrestrials have concrete messages for him:

> Because of the information I obtained, I started to paint. I never learned to paint, but all of a sudden I could just do it. So I made a number of *cosmic paintings,* and I give lectures about them. The purpose of all this is to prepare mankind for the presence and the arrival of the extraterrestrials. I do realize this sounds crazy and fantastic, and people don't have to believe me as long as they just bear it in mind. And there is more information, which is not so positive, namely, that there is much going on with our natural environment, much worse than most people suspect. In that respect many ill-considered activities take place by the people and their governments, even in such a way that humanity is actually in danger. That is another reason for me to give lectures, so that I can warn people about that.

According to Bob, many more contacts from the cosmos will take place in our time.

> In the near future more and more information will come to us this way. And in fact, I meet more and more other people who have had experiences similar to mine. Often they do not know how to cope with it, but I try to help them and put them on the right track. Because people are just people, and sometimes they don't interpret the messages correctly. What I mean is that sometimes the messages are misused for their own fame and glory. But

we should never forget one thing: We are just instruments, *media,* nothing more.

The message of the crop circles, according to Bob, is simple. "Crop circles are a way to show the people that there is also life outside the earth. That is the only intention of crop circles, to make us experience that we are not alone in this universe." Bob also has an understanding about how crop circles are made. "One way is that a ball moves over the fields. And just a few moments later a circle or a formation of circles is created." Despite this very summary explanation, it is interesting to realize that this statement about a "ball" dates from a time in which the crop circle–related BOLs were not such a current topic as they are today.

Bob is also convinced that the crop circle phenomenon has not yet come to an end. "I expect an increase in the number of crop circles, with the purpose to show us that we are not the only ones, and the final goal of all this is the acquaintance with our brothers from space, the extraterrestrials."

Gate to Another World

A COUPLE OF YEARS AGO I MET JAAP VAN ETTEN, WHO HAS BEEN ENGAGED for years in the study of earth energies and *ley lines.* Ley lines are alleged "energetic channels" running over and in the earth's crust and making up a worldwide network of "floating energy." One day he told me about a revealing experience during a vacation in Mexico. While visiting the ancient Mayan pyramids, he used his divining rod to localize a "strong energetic" spot, where he decided to stay for meditation. Soon he obtained, as he said, "a vision of another world."

> It was as if I could see through our own existing world, into another dimension, or perhaps I should say: see through a dimension into another world. I could see land, plants, trees, and large pyramids, surrounded by energies of various colors. After a while I noticed how I could only receive these images in particular locations, nowhere else, as if on those spots there were a sort of gates allowing access to that other world.

Later that year, he visited a crop formation that had appeared in the south of the Netherlands. Much to his astonishment, standing in the crop circle he experienced exactly the same thing that had happened earlier, in Mexico. Again, images from another world came through, this time including people, and again with large pyramids, surrounded by energies of various colors. And just as in Mexico, this experience seemed to be tied to a particular area, namely, the physical imprint of the crop formation. Only there could the experience be invoked, and not outside the formation. It seemed as if the crop circle formed a window that allowed the human mind to receive a glimpse of another world, or as if the crop circle acted as a point of contact between two different worlds, ours and another one. Could it be possible that the curious phenomena observed in and around crop circles, such as unidentified balls of light and strange deposits, are actually originating from this "parallel world"? Could it be possible that the circle creators themselves come from this world? Could it be possible that the transdimensional connection between two "parallel worlds" is accompanied by disturbances of the progress of time as we experience it? That would explain the reports of watches and other electronic equipment acting up in crop circles.

In his excellent book *Vital Signs* the British crop circle researcher Andy Thomas describes a photograph of a crop circle showing a double exposure artifact only at the position of the crop circle, and not elsewhere. The people standing inside the formation appear twice on the photograph, slightly shifted, and apparently at two different moments in time (separated by about a second?) as indicated by the slightly different poses. However, the artifact could not be explained by simply assuming a double exposure, because at the edges the photograph was perfectly normal! Thomas suggested that perhaps time itself got disturbed inside the pictogram, so that two different moments in time inside the formation appeared as one single moment by the time the optical shutter of the camera opened. This is a daring hypothesis, but then again, even after careful studies nobody else has come up with a trivial explanation.

Over the years many people have told me that they have had a feeling someone was watching them whenever they entered a crop circle, even if they were obviously the only person for miles around. "I feel like a germ then," someone once said to me, "and the crop circle is the microscope. It feels like every step I make inside the formation is carefully monitored by someone or something." Many others have told me that they feel strongly connected to the Circlemakers, whoever they are, whenever they are inside the circles. Perhaps they would see colored pyramids too, if they were more susceptible?

Messages from the Cosmos

IN 1997, THE DUTCH ORGANIZATION FRONTIER SCIENCES FOUNDATION organized a crop circle symposium, at which the British researcher Andy Thomas and I each gave a lecture. As usual, after the presentations there were many questions from the audience. After some twenty minutes, because of time constraints, the chairman assigned the last question to a middle-aged woman.

"I don't know how to say this," she started, hesitating, "but I am clairvoyant and I was told to bring a message to all of you at this symposium."

A short silence followed, after which she continued: "I have to say that it will not be long before the meaning of the crop circles will be clear to everyone." That was it. There was no time left to go more deeply into this statement, and while I translated the woman's words into English for Andy, the chairman closed the conference.

One year later, shortly after I had published my previous crop circle book,[3] I received a letter from the same woman. Her name was Riet de Graaf, and she told me that she was paranormally gifted, worked as a healer, and had received a message through clairvoyance that she had to purchase a newly published book about crop circles (which was my book). After she obtained a copy, she was told to translate the pictograms with the aid of a pendulum and a letter board. She wrote that she was completely taken aback by the translations that had appeared. The letter ended, "I have my feet firmly on the ground, but there is more between heaven and earth, and the time is ripe." Because I had just decided to approach the crop circle phenomenon not exclusively from a scientific point of view, but sometimes also completely without any rationalism, I decided to call the woman and made an appointment for a visit. And so it happened that, a few days later, I was sitting in my study browsing through a long list of diagrams taken from my book, accompanied by her translation for each of them. The translations consisted of curious single sentences, many of them talking about "cosmic beings" and "reforming" or "helping the world." A few examples are given here.

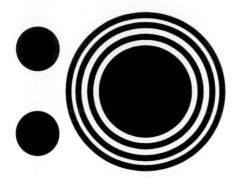

"A cosmic creature is on earth and is coming to the people" (part of the Alton Barnes formation, England, 1990).

"A young soul will come to help us" (part of the Bratton Castle formation, England, 1990).

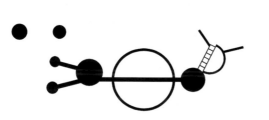

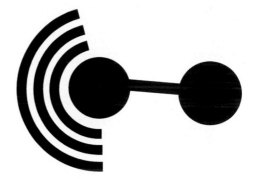

"A long day and a long night" (Litchfield, England, 1991).

"A beautiful cosmic man" (Telegraph Hill, England, 1990).

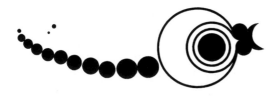

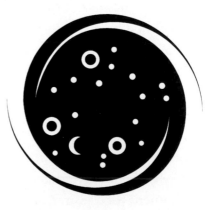

"A long night with much misery" (Bishops Cannings, England, 1994).

"A cosmic being with extensive information and much knowledge" (West Stowell, England,

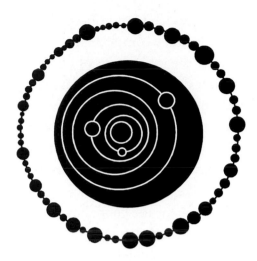

"Soon there will be a great change to the world" (Colmont, Holland, 1996).

"A cosmic story with a good end" (Winchester, England, 1995).

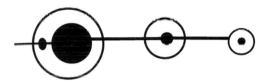

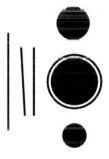

"A cosmic universe with much motion and much clarification" (Landgraaf, Holland, 1996).

"A beautiful entity and a beautiful new start" (Zuid-Limburg, Holland, 1996).

Although the individual phrases were interesting, I did not have any idea how to extract a clear and consistent message from them. However, this message was given more explicitly during one of my next visits to Riet, when she told me about her regular (clairvoyant) communications with entities she called "cosmic masters" and "intelligences." Among them are Master Kuna, Master John, Master Theodore, and, according to Riet's firm conviction, no less than the Archangel Michael, Jesus Christ, and even God himself. I do realize that some people might be offended by such a statement, but I am only the messenger. Moreover, doesn't the Bible describe how in ancient times people also used to talk to God in person?

At the beginning of each month, Riet receives messages from the Archangel Michael and other intelligences, which she carefully compiles and prints with her computer. The messages make clear that the inhabitants of Planet Earth are carefully watched by entities beyond our daily perception, who are sympathetic toward us. Perhaps these are the same entities that have been recorded in the Bible as "angels," perhaps they are the spirits of our deceased ancestors, or perhaps they are entities completely beyond our imagination. Whatever their origin, it is clear to Riet that these entities are preoccupied with us, because they expect major changes to take place on earth, in the short term. I don't know if these changes will only be for the good; however, Riet's messages clearly indicate that during the course of events, love, consideration, modesty, and self-consciousness will bring us much benefit.

True or False?

AFTER READING THE PREVIOUS SECTIONS OF THIS CHAPTER, WHICH FORM quite a contrast with the rest of the book, I can hear you think: "Do you believe all of this yourself?" My answer is simple: I don't know. But I also think it does not matter. Over the years, I have learned that psychic "predictions" (or at least their interpretations) are often not very accurate. The "King of Terror descending from heavens" in July 1999, as predicted by Nostradamus, and the Great Pole Shift (the tumbling of the earth axis) on May 5, 2000, are just two simple examples. Nevertheless, I think it is important never to *exclude* the possibility of something that might be very significant one day, no matter how strange it seems. It is clear that no rational arguing will help us here, since we are confronted with a (per definition) nonrational concept. But we can always try to distinguish between the essentials and the side issues. Is the main consideration the question if they are all true, and the side issue the question if the insights can help us? Or is it exactly the other way round: The main issue is if the insights can serve us somehow, no matter if they are based on the truth or not? I guess the answer to this question is simple. Consequently, the "true or not true" dilemma does not bother me a lot. Nevertheless, there is one event I would like to tell you about, because it would immediately have convinced many skeptics if it had happened to them. During one of my visits to Riet, another "cosmic entity" revealed himself.

"Oh, this is nice," Riet said. "This is very nice." She put down her pendulum and looked me in the eyes.

"They want to bless you," she said. "That does not happen a lot. You should be happy, you will receive a cosmic blessing." She pointed at the fountain pen in my hand.

"You'd better put that down and relax. Just relax, with your hands open on the table. And just wait."

Not knowing what to expect, I did as I was told. I closed my eyes and tried to relax.

"Sometimes, when this happens, you can feel it," I heard Riet say. She had hardly finished her words when I felt my abdominal muscles cramp together as if there were an electrical current flowing through them. A strong tingling sensation spread from my stomach to my back, my shoulders, toward my head, down my arms, and also down to my legs. It was an indescribable feeling, not unpleasant, a sort of strong, itchy shiver. The sensation resembled the feeling I remember from childhood, for example, when I played hide and seek with an adult who was very close, pretending not to see me. A combination of excitement, happiness, and great fun. (Later, I realized how Robbert had said the same thing: "This happy feeling, like you have when you are a kid, the day before your birthday or so. A most exciting feeling, somewhere around your stomach.") It lasted about half a minute, after which my muscles relaxed and the shivers slowly disappeared.

"Now that you have received this cosmic blessing, you will never fall ill anymore," Riet said.

That night, returned from the spiritual spheres, I described to my neighbor how explicit and real the experience had been: "If they had hit me on the head with a frying pan it couldn't have been clearer!"

Without doubt, some will nevertheless say that this was all just a matter of imagination or self-illusion. Perhaps they are right, although at the time this seemed highly unlikely to me. And the curious fact is, although it is common in my environment to catch a virus at least several times a year, since the event (over three years ago by now) I have not even caught the slightest cold. Would that be just coincidence?

Notes

1. The word *energy* is used rather loosely here, as is usual in discussions of the paranormal, and should not be confused with the formal, scientific definition of energy.

2. See note 1 above.

3. *Het Raadsel van de Graancirkels, Feiten, Analysen, Hypothesen* (The Crop Circle Enigma, Facts, Analyses, Hypotheses) Deventer: Ankh-Hermes, 1998. Published in Dutch only.

Kennewick, USA, 1993.
Photograph © ilyes.

Chehalis, USA, 1994.

Photograph © ilyes.

Chehalis, USA, 1994. This photograph was taken after harvest, when young seedlings (from seeds that had fallen out of the flattened crop) made the pictogram reappear.

Photograph © ilyes.

Bishop's Cannings, England, 2000.
Photograph © Bert Janssen.

Hakpen Hill, England, 1999.
Photograph © Dr. Andrew King.

Silbury Hill, England, 2000. Note how one of the small triangles is out of place! Although it was suggested that this was the result of digital editing of original photographs, the formation was actually made this way. The reason of this strange design aspect has obviously been the subject of countless discussions. Photograph © Bert Janssen.

Chapter 5

Circular Arguments

Although many issues surrounding crop circles have not been discussed, the most important ones have been addressed. Good discussions about any topic should end with a number of conclusions. This chapter will look back on several issues discussed earlier and put them in perspective. Where necessary, additional information will be presented as well.

The Clash

IT WILL BE CLEAR TO YOU BY NOW THAT THE ORIGIN OF MANY CROP CIRCLES is in fact still a big question for any serious researcher. Simple issues about them have never been explained satisfactorily. Many will claim the opposite and make statements such as, "It has been shown many times that all crop circles are just the work of human pranksters. It has been shown on TV and broadcast all over the world. There is no mystery at all." However, these statements are always based on a lack of factual knowledge (if not on evil intent). Whenever someone comes up with these types of arguments, I always ask for foundation or a solid reference. No one has ever given me one. Apparently, there is a desperate need for denial of the facts. And this is not strange, because crop circles seem to defy any plausible, simple explanation, which is very frustrating in our times, as there always seems to be an answer to everything. However, the true mystery aspect of crop circles is not in their tremendous complexity, their enormous dimensions, or the vast number of reported formations (about ten thousand since the late seventies, which corresponds to one almost every day). I am convinced that even the most advanced pattern could have been designed and produced by a well-prepared, motivated, and intelligent group of people, with relatively simple tools. I am not saying that it is easy, and it will mean lots and lots of work, but it can be done. I think I could do it myself, if I could afford the time to become good at it (and had a good team of assistants with me, of course). We all know that there are several groups of hoaxers active, particularly in the south of England, and although I believe that their role is overestimated, we know they make crop circles, and they like to fool people.

The true mystery of crop circles is also not in the thousands of experiments reporting unusual biophysical anomalies, and not even in the balls of light, for which solid physical evidence has been given in Chapter Three of this book. Although many, if not most of the reported (bio-) physical anomalies are not yet understood, they might be explained as side effects of a yet unknown natural phenomenon, perhaps a brand-new one induced by the rapid environmental changes of our world, such as global heating, the greenhouse effect, the thinning ozone layer, and the ever-increasing pollution. Much work will have to be done before the mechanism of, for example, BOLs and their relationship with crop circles will become clear. However, the observations of structured node lengthening, germination anomalies, and perhaps even the video footage of BOLs give us at least a handle, something we can start to work on. It does not lead us to a dead end right away.

We can postulate plausible hypotheses, assuming that the BOLs emit a combination of infrared radiation and ionizing radiation, with much shorter wavelengths. The infrared (or perhaps microwave radiation) would heat up the stems, causing structured node lengthening, while the shorter wavelengths would change the chemical composition and molecular structure of the seeds in the seedheads, leading to germination anomalies. The hypothesis does not explain where the BOLs come from and how they are created, nor does it explain the exact mechanism of the germination anomalies. But at least it is a start, with enough degrees of freedom for the next steps of research to a new, unknown natural phenomenon.

This vision was shared by Dr. Terence Meaden, who concluded in the early nineties that the circular imprints in crop fields were the effect of a natural phenomenon, plasma vortices, while all the advanced geometric designs must be the work of hoaxers. This sounds perfectly right. However, the *clash* comes when we discover that exactly the same physical and biophysical anomalies explained in Chapter Three of this book also manifest themselves in the noncircular, advanced geometric designs, such as, for example, the Stonehenge formation,[1] discussed in Chapter One of this book, the Melick formation, discussed in Chapter Three,[2] and literally hundreds of other complex pictograms with intricate geometry investigated by the BLT team. Ninety percent of the investigated formations revealed germination anomalies, cellular anomalies, structured, nonbiologic node length increase, and so on. Isn't it incredible that, even after scientific publication of these findings, there are still people who simply dismiss the crop circle phenomenon as the work of human pranksters with a garden roller?

As the designs of these crop pictograms most obviously reveal a fair amount of intelligence, it is implausible that they are the result of a natural phenomenon. It has been suggested that nature itself also produces intricate geometric patterns, such as snow crystals. This argument might (perhaps?) be valid to suggest an explanation for diatonic ratios, discussed in Chapter Three. There are many examples for the self-reproduction of physical phenomena on different, well-determined scales, for example, sound waves with higher harmonics. However, this argument won't stand up when one considers the Milk Hill formation of 1997 (see page v), which was a clear representation of a Koch fractal, a non-natural, mathematical concept invented by the German mathematician Von Koch in the early part of the twentieth century. And hundreds, if not thousands of other designs have been reported, lacking even the faintest similarity to anything we know in nature. So are these all made by people with planks and ropes, as Dr. Meaden suggested? If the answer to that question were yes, why then do they reveal the same biophysical anomalies as the simple round circles do? And why do they show construction lines underneath the flattened crop that do not extend into the standing crop, although they cannot be made without reference points outside the flattened area, as discussed in Chapter Three? Why is the crop undamaged, even in oil seed rape, a plant so brittle that you can almost break the stems by just looking at them? Indeed, there are dozens of other valid questions one could ask that preclude a simple explanation for crop circle phenomena.

> Conclusion One: The suggestion that crop circles are all made by practical jokers with simple flattening tools is by no means sufficient to explain all documented observations.

Electromagnetism—Or Not?

MANY OTHER RESEARCHERS HAVE REPORTED INDICATIONS OF THE involvement of electromagnetism in the formation of crop circles. Electromagnetism refers to magnetic fields (as created by, e.g., a simple bar magnet), electrostatic fields (which cause the crackling sound when you comb your hair), or electromagnetic waves (radio waves, heat radiation, light, UV radiation, X-rays, etc.). All of these have been reported in crop circles by many different researchers, sometimes by performing well-designed experiments, other times by just mentioning the presence of "abnormally high magnetic values," whatever that may mean. The node length analysis presented in Chapter Three of this book, and in particular the linear regression analysis on one of the sample sets, were further indications of the electromagnetic character of a ball of light, which, according to an eyewitness, created a crop circle. Crop circles, however, seem to have the nasty habit of contradicting any hypothesis as soon as it is presented. Just such a contradiction happened with respect to the suggested electromagnetic "fingerprint" in crop formations.

In the early summer of 1999 I visited a simple circle in a potato field near the village of Sevenum, Holland. In a perfect circle with a diameter of seven meters, the potato plants had collapsed on the ground. Interestingly, they were not squeezed against the ground, as often observed in corn-type plants, but just hanging down, sort of flabby. The ground was soft and brittle, and clearly showed my own footprints. No other footprints or any evidence of human activity were found. Closer inspection revealed that parts of the stems of the plants had been dehydrated. It was yet another demonstration of heat effects involved in crop circle formation; however, this time there was a curious complication. I noticed how the stems were only locally dehydrated, from close above the ground to about five centimeters higher. At that point all dry, thin, and floppy stems showed an abrupt boundary, from which the plants seemed untouched. This can be seen in Figure 5-1. Note how in the center of the yellow circle the stem is a light brown color (dehydrated), while halfway toward the left the color suddenly changes (here the stem was still full of water).

The same thing can be seen elsewhere in the photograph, while all the

Figure 5-1. Local dehydration of potato plant stems. Note my footprint (top right) in the soft and brittle ground.

plants in the circle showed the same characteristics: Dehydration had taken place in a circular pattern, from just above the soil to about five centimeters higher. If this dehydration were the effect of electromagnetic radiation, its energy was confined in what scientists call a "pillbox," a closed, circularly symmetric volume of finite height. The radiation could not have come from above, because in that case the plants would have been dehydrated all the way down from their tops. It could also not have come from the sides, because then it would never have created a perfect circle with a sharp boundary. However, a fundamental property of electromagnetic radiation is that it cannot be confined in a pillbox shape without such a pillbox actually being there! The only way in which electromagnetic radiation can be stored in any volume is by creating an electrically conducting wall around that volume. It will never happen in open air. So whatever caused the dehydration of these potato plants, it was definitely not of the same character as the BOL that created the crop circle discussed in Chapter Three. The only way in which the potato plants could have been dehydrated the way they were is one plant at a time, by a very local heat or radiation source, operating from a short distance. Actually, this finding gives an underpinning for one of the accounts by the young Dutchman, mentioned in Chapter One. He said: "Balls of light, spinning very rapidly through the crop, so that it almost resembled a fluorescent disk." Supposing these balls were able to cause dehydration (which is possible, since they were emitting bright light so they could be hot), then you would indeed expect an end result as found in this potato field: the trace of a round disk, just above the ground, with finite thickness. So once again, a curious and apparently fantastic eyewitness account seems to be backed up by simple observations and some straightforward physics.

Pseudoscientists

THE TERM *pseudoscientist* IS USED QUITE OFTEN IN CROP CIRCLE-RELATED discussions, usually in the less friendly ones. Interestingly, the term is also employed by nonscientists, accusing scientists of—in their opinion—inaccurate procedures or methods and false conclusions. To be labeled a pseudoscientist requires only that you talk about crop circles and don't dismiss them as the work of practical jokers with planks and ropes. This simple fact makes you a pseudoscientist in the eyes of many! Beware!

Imagination, creative and unconventional thinking are quickly considered as nonscientific heresy, although we all know that the great scientists of the past (Albert Einstein, Max Planck, Niels Bohr, Erwin Schrödinger, to name just a few) were all highly unconventional thinkers. They all showed that, in order to expand the domain of science, it is sometimes important to let go of all traditional ideas and just radically jump over the cliff of conventional theories. Most of the time, the results are not noteworthy. But sometimes these people came back to the world of traditional science with great ideas and new insights, which later resulted in rigorous improvements of scientific theories. Nevertheless, many scientists always meticulously stay behind the fence that stakes out the territory of traditional Western science, and never even look at the other side. At the same time, the physical models that have been

> Conclusion Two: The crop circle phenomenon is often erroneously ridiculed, and much underestimated in its complexity.

developed, and which only act as tools to structure our thinking in order to describe, predict, and control our observations of the reality around us, are identified with this reality itself. Consequently, all that does not fit in the model, all that is on the other side of the fence, cannot exist and is dismissed as nonsense, nonscientific twaddle, or pseudoscience. An approach to reasoning that is similarly flawed.

Nevertheless, although an open mind and the ability to think without conventional constraints are excellent virtues, it is extremely important that you always know exactly where your thoughts and ideas should be positioned with respect to the established science. It is all right to jump over the fence of traditionalism, as long as you can find your way back. There are many ideas and theories I know, which I never could (and never will) employ in my daily activities as a scientist. Science is a game, and if you want to play it well, you have to stick to the rules. When you play baseball, you are not allowed to hit the ball with a tennis racket. But that does not mean that someone who likes to play tennis can never be a good baseball player.

This concept, however, is not accepted by everybody. Many people believe that once you take such a controversial subject as crop circles seriously, you are a pseudoscientist and consequently cannot think at all. They will say your thinking is unscientific and consider this as a fatal disease; once you have had these sinful, unscientific thoughts, you can never be cured again. But there are many ways of thinking, and even many ways of scientific thinking. For me, science is like a cap. When I go to work, I put it on. When I work on crop circles, I sometimes put it on, and sometimes take it off. When I play my guitar, I always take it off. But perhaps others have the caps glued to their heads?

> Conclusion Three: The true nature of the crop circle phenomenon is unknown to the general public.

Good and Bad Critics

As I noted earlier, much of the criticism of crop circles is based on factual ignorance. Most of it is not objective either, and not based on a careful analysis of facts. Although there are definitely crop circle "believers," intrigued by the unknown and so emotionally involved that they are willing to accept anything as long as it adds to the mystery, a similar attitude can be observed with many of the skeptics. They start their reasoning from the conclusion: Crop circles are simply made by men with simple tools. Next, they will blindly attack any argument that indicates the opposite. Germination anomalies are based on a wild imagination and inaccurate procedures, videos and eyewitnesses of BOLs are based on fraud, and node-length measurements were done by manipulation of the statistics. It is interesting how the critics hardly ever take the trouble to actually verify results obtained by others and never perform their own experiments to show the opposite. Their activities are usually limited to short articles. The British researcher Busty Taylor once referred to these persons as "armchair critics," a very appropriate expression indeed.

Nevertheless, I believe that critics should not just be considered as a burden. I will always be open to all criticism related to my work on crop circles (and beyond), because it acts as a free "ordeal" for all my experiments and findings. I am not afraid to be proven wrong by anybody. On the contrary, I want to be sure that my findings are correct, and that I can convince myself in the first place. Any critical remark made by skeptics might help me to get closer to an answer.

On the other hand, sometimes the criticisms by skeptics are not only ill-considered, but even completely ridiculous. There are several articles about me in which I have been called an "idiot" chasing "little green men who create patterns in the fields." Such articles are written by people with whom I never spoke and who do not know anything about me or my work. I wonder what drives them. (Those more paranoid than I suggest that these people are hired by the government as part of a worldwide coverup, so as to ridicule serious researchers who have become aware of something strange going on.) The television interview with the video-editing forgery, which apparently made me say things that I would not even *think,* is another example of the chicanery that sometimes reveals itself. Apparently, some people are so convinced of their unfounded ideas that they stop at nothing in order to tell the world. The crop circle researcher *must* be crazy, and if they can't find any indication to support their opinion, they simply create one!

Conclusion Four: "Those who are unqualified to judge should refrain from comment" (Dr. G. Terence Meaden)

The Wrong Question

THE THEME OF MOST ARTICLES THAT HAVE BEEN WRITTEN ABOUT CROP CIRCLES is: *Are they made by humans or not?* This, however, is the wrong question, which immediately follows from its consequences. Crop circles clearly show an impressive intelligence in their design. So if they are not made by humans, who makes them? Animals? Not likely. So what other intelligence can be responsible? There is only one answer left. The question "made by humans or not" only seems to leave room for wild, *Star Trek*–style speculations about extraterrestrials, flying saucers, government conspiracies, and so on. Such speculation, which automatically follows, guarantees the attention of the reader and brings the article to an exciting level. It also makes a nice contrast with the plot: the introduction of a group of human pranksters who made a crop circle with the aid of a plank or a garden roller. Articles like these appear every year in the newspapers, accompanied by slogans such as, "This story will forever change your view on the crop circle phenomenon." They almost seem to be an intermittent drug to keep the public ignorant. But who knows, perhaps crop circles are indeed made by men, only not with the aid of ropes, garden rollers, or planks, but with much more sophisticated equipment. It all shows how limited the question "humans or not" is, simply because it is the wrong question. If you ask the wrong question, you will get wrong answers.

A correct question would be: "How are crop circles made?" And the reasons for asking this question are the observations presented in this book. These observations are unambiguous, they are made repeatedly, they are very curious, and they have not been explained yet. Since almost nobody in the world actually knows about this, these simple facts ought to be discussed first, before one plunges into discussions about extraterrestrials. Although speculation about intelligent life beyond our planet is extremely exciting, there have never been explicit indications from the crop circles leading to conclusions in that direction. This does not mean that crop circles cannot be made by an extraterrestrial intelligence. Obviously, this hypothesis cannot be refuted. However, it has also never been proven, which makes it of little use to take the matter into consideration until clear indications present themselves. Until then, there will be more than enough work to clarify the non-speculative issues about crop circles.

The Facts

IN THE LAST TWENTY YEARS, THERE HAS BEEN MUCH SPECULATION ABOUT different aspects of crop circles. But it takes more than just a little reading to understand where the facts end and where the fiction begins. Personal involvement and investigations, field work, discussions with many people, critical questions, and much thinking are needed to reveal the true character of the crop circle phenomenon. Unfortunately, much of the public information is not very accurate or even is completely wrong, as a result of ignorance, lack of accuracy or objectivity, or simply evil intent. Although many alleged crop circle properties cannot bear the scrutiny of an objective analysis, some relatively simple observations seem to defy any trivial explanation. Biophysical anomalies, in terms of node lengthening and germination anomalies, are probably number one on this list. The lack of any indication of human presence or mechanical flattening, observed many times in even the most fragile and delicate species of crop, is perhaps somewhat less objective but still good for a second place. The awesome complexity and particularly the hidden geometry in many of the pictograms at least indicate that this cannot all be the result of a simple joke. Even fantastic and extraordinary observations, in the form of a radiant ball of light hovering above a field and creating a crop circle, can fulfill the requirement that "extraordinary claims require extraordinary evidence." This extraordinary evidence was delivered in Chapter Three. The node-length measurements unambiguously showed a perfect symmetry in three different cross sections through the circular imprint, in perfect correlation with the radiation pattern of an electromagnetic point source. This is indeed the required extraordinary evidence, which at least ought to open our minds to the dozens of other, similar eyewitness accounts, and of course the video material of the flying balls of light. Moreover, since identical findings were accepted for publication in the scientific literature, it is quite legitimate to say that the involvement of balls of light in crop circle formation has by now become a scientifically accepted fact.[3] And there is much more extraordinary evidence, in the form of burn marks on the bird box; delicately draped, undamaged carrot leaves; a virgin circle in a frozen field of snow; dead flies, and much more. Anyone who takes the time to explore and verify all of these findings personally will find that the facts are plain: Something very strange is going on.

> Conclusion Five: Small radiation sources with an electromagnetic character ("Balls of Light") are directly involved in the creation of crop circles. (Their origin and exact character remain yet unknown.)

So Where Do They Come From?

THIS, OF COURSE, IS THE QUESTION THAT EVERYBODY ASKS. NOW THAT YOU are almost at the end of this book, you will understand that the answer cannot be so easily found. The only firm conclusion we can reach so far is that the suggestion that crop circles are all made by practical jokers with planks and ropes (or other simple flattening tools) is by no means sufficient to explain all documented observations. This is not a hypothesis; it is a fact. It is also an important conclusion, which should stimulate further study into the crop circle phenomenon.

Nevertheless, a few considerations with respect to the origin of crop circles may be suggested. It has come to my attention that crop circles can be divided into at least three different types, as if there are at least three different sources that create them.

The first type are the simple, round circles, as were reported in the "Mowing Devil" account, as were seen by several eyewitnesses throughout the early part of the twentieth century, and as appeared in increasing numbers in the south of England during the late seventies and early eighties. They have continued to appear to this very day, worldwide. It is interesting to note that, as far as I know, all alleged eyewitnesses who saw a crop circle appear before their eyes witnessed the appearance of only these simple, round formations. Some eyewitnesses have seen how a number of circles appear simultaneously, and although there are several reports of complex geometric formations that apparently appeared in a very short time, to my knowledge no one has ever witnessed the actual appearance of such a sophisticated pictogram. Consequently, all eyewitness reports including the involvement of balls of light during the creation of a crop circle are also limited to the simple round ones.

These facts seem to support the hypothesis by Dr. Terence Meaden, who already suggested in the eighties that crop circles are the result of an air current from the upper atmosphere, accompanied by luminous, electric effects.

The second type of crop circle is the "circles-rings-and-bars" type, as first recorded in the south of England in 1990 and several years later in the rest of the world. The Melick formation discussed in Chapter Three and Appendix C was of this type. Personally, I think this second type is the most curious one. Despite their relatively simple appearance, these pictograms have revealed an incredibly complex geometry. Although this does not indicate that they cannot be man-made, they do raise many valid questions regarding how and why. Unlike the many beautiful, intricate works of "crop art," of which the complexity is crystal clear at a first glance, these "circles-rings-and-bars" formations have their complexity deeply hidden inside the design, to be revealed only by those with enough spare time and enough knowledge of mathematics. The shapes and patterns of these pictograms are in fact "mystical," and look like a sort of strange, written symbolic language. Although this suggestion is highly speculative, of course, many people seem to feel the same.

I would not be surprised if the largest number of human hoaxes can be found in the fantastic, intricate, highly complicated, and eye-catching formations that appear every year in the south of England. This is the third type. Most of these crop formations have some sort of circular symmetry, like a mandala, and the fact that they all seem to be designed for their mere beauty make them a good candidate for pieces of "landscape art," as some hoaxers like to call their work.

Of course it is difficult, if not impossible, to define the borderline between one type of crop formation and another, and many examples cannot be classified into any of the three types I mentioned here. But the different types of crop circles and the different "characters" they seem to reveal leads one to suspect that not all crop circles are made by one and the same entity. There must be several sources. As mentioned earlier, the "clash" comes when biophysical anomalies are found in the advanced geometrical formations. Perhaps this can be explained by assuming that hoaxers enhance the simple round formations into the more elaborate patterns. However, even this suggestion leaves many questions unanswered. The ever-increasing complexity of the formations in combination with the frequent absence of any traces of human activity is only one of them. Future research should therefore be directed to the abundant sampling of these geometric patterns, followed by well-established biophysical tests such as node-length measurements and seed germination trials, in a similar fashion as presented in Chapter Three. The amount of work involved, however, will be much more than for a simple round circle, and one may wonder how many scientists will be able to perform such a time-consuming study without any financing or other compensation.

Public Awareness

BY NOW YOU HAVE LEARNED THE TRUE NATURE OF THE CROP CIRCLE PHEnomenon in its full complexity. I hope you agree that the subject is very interesting. However, I want to emphasize that this book is just an open and honest account of my personal findings and thoughts. As noted earlier, it is certainly not my intention to *defend* crop circles as being a phenomenon without a trivial explanation. I do not insist. All I do is observe, and admit that I have not yet found satisfactory answers to many questions that I have encountered during my years of circle hunting. I am also not trying to convince anyone, because people will have to convince themselves, by a critical and objective approach, by personal involvement, and by thinking for themselves—not by just blindly accepting what others tell them. I do hope that the findings I have published in this book will stimulate others to verify the results by performing similar experiments, as I was stimulated (or perhaps a little suspicious?) by the results published by the BLT team. When enough people have become involved this way and have become convinced by personal experience that crop circles are worth paying attention to, perhaps a "critical mass" can be reached, which will bring crop circle studies to a higher level. And this is necessary, because it will take more than a handful of scientists and crop circle enthusiasts to solve the puzzle. Much more research will be needed, and funds will have to be raised.

Obviously, I think it would be a good thing to do. Not only because crop circles are a highly interesting phenomenon, but also because it might actually be very important to understand their meaning and their origin, because they have continued to appear for such a long time, more and more intensively every year. Moreover, it has been scientifically shown that crop circles cause biological changes to the seeds of grain-type plants. Even radioactivity has been measured inside crop circles. So someone or something is manipulating our daily bread, without our permission, and without anyone knowing what on earth is going on. Since a combine harvester cannot tell the difference between the normal and the circle seeds, this means that the manipulated seeds have already entered our food chain a long time ago and ended up in our bread, pasta, biscuits, and lots of other food, which is consumed by all of us. Think about this next time you eat a sandwich or a slice of pizza.

Isn't it the responsibility of all of us to try to find out what is happening? If our governments would just take a few pennies per family (which is a negligible amount of the tax money we all pay) and spend it on crop circle research, imagine the things that could be accomplished and the progress that could be made. Imagine how many things could be discovered in a short time. How many *exciting* things, perhaps. Unfortunately, we are not at that point yet. Creating the proper public awareness is a first hurdle before anything else will occur. If our awareness remains at today's low level, and as long as ill-considered arguments about crop circles are swallowed by the public without any further thinking, not a lot will happen. Wouldn't that be a shame? Well, that is exactly the reason I decided to write this book.

> Conclusion Six: Something very strange is going on.

Notes

1. BLT report 78, 1996.

2. I performed some simple germination tests with seeds taken from this formation and discovered moderate but statistically relevant germination retardation. More surprising was the fact that the seedlings from the crop circle lasted almost two weeks without water, while the controls all died within a week. Similar findings had been observed earlier by Levengood.

3. E. H. Haselhoff, "Dispersion of Energies in Worldwide Crop Formations" (Opinions and Comments), *Physiologia Plantarum* 111, vol. 1 (2000): 124.

The magnificent "Crown" of Devizes, England, 1999.
Photograph © Ron Russell.

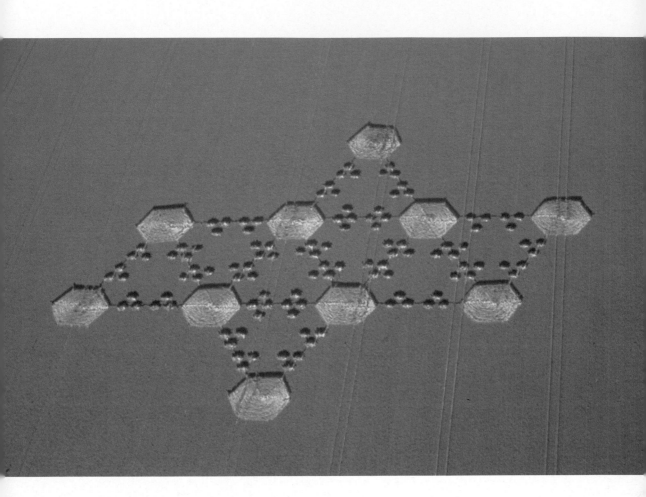

West Overton, England, 1999.

Photograph © Ron Russell.

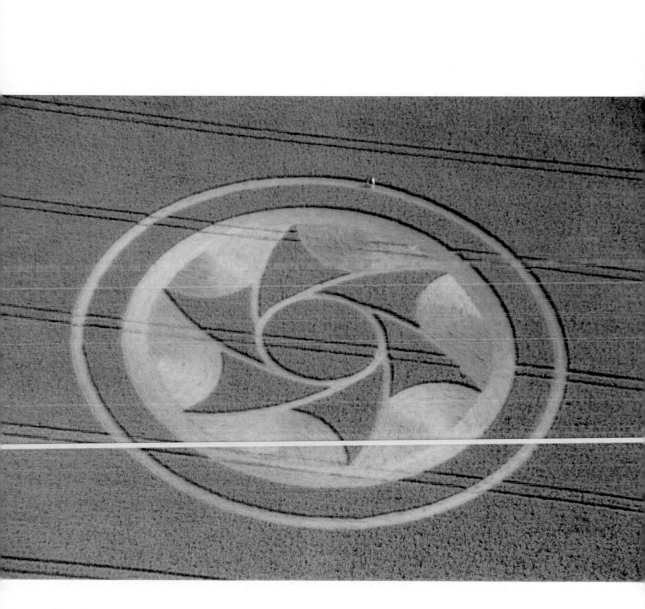

Etchilhampton, England, 1999. Despite its relatively simple appearance, the design of this pictogram is based on advanced mathematics.
Photograph © Dr. Andrew King.

East Kennett, England, 2000.
Photograph © Janet Ossebaard.

Adam's Grave, England, 2000.
Photograph © Bert Janssen.

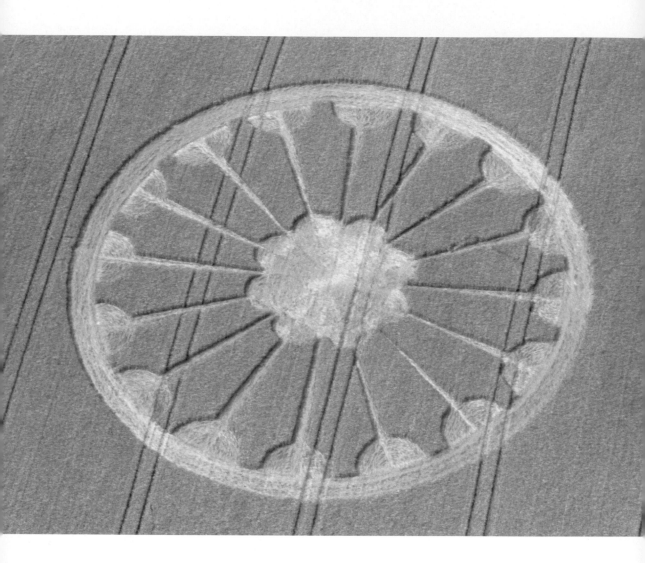

South Field, England, 2000.

Photograph © Janet Ossebaard.

Diatonic Ratios

THE CENTRAL C KEY ON A PIANO KEYBOARD (ALSO CALLED *do*) CORRESPONDS to a tone with a frequency of 264 hertz (Hz, vibrations per second). This means that the piano strings, after the central C key is played, will move back and forth 264 times per second, producing an acoustic wave in the air with the same frequency. The tones corresponding to the white keys to the right of the central C, denoted by D-E-F-G-A-B-C (or simply *re-fa-sol-la-ti-do*), have frequencies with very specific proportions, called diatonic ratios. These are listed below:

1	9/8	5/4	4/3	3/2	5/3	15/8	2
C	D	E	F	G	A	B	C'
do	re	mi	fa	so	la	ti	do

The frequency of the E note is consequently 5/4 times higher than the frequency of the central C, corresponding to 330 Hz. The G has a frequency of 3/2 x 264 = 396 Hz, and so on. With fretted instruments, like a guitar or a banjo, another method of tuning is employed. On these instruments the frequency of the tones increases exponentially (this is called a tempered scale). In this case the frequencies can be written as a rational power of two, written as $2^{n/12}$, where *n* equals one of the following values:

0	2	4	5	7	9	11	12
C	D	E	F	G	A	B	C'
do	re	m	fa	so	la	ti	do

The frequencies of the tempered scale are hence not identical to the frequencies of the diatonic scale, but it takes a well-developed ear for music to notice the difference.

Like the diatonic ratios of a musical scale, the geometrical ratios of crop circle formations were expressed by Gerald Hawkins also in terms of the exponential expression $2^{n/12}$, after which he evaluated the corresponding values of n. If the diameters of the crop circles had been arbitrary, arbitrary values of n would have been found. However, only values corresponding closely to 0, 2, 4, 5, 7, 9, 11, and 12 were determined, exactly matching the white keys of a piano keyboard. The numbers corresponding to the black keys, 1, 3, 6, 8, and 10, were never found.

The Isosceles Triangle Theorem

CONSIDER A CIRCLE C_1 WITH RADIUS EQUAL TO 1 (ONE), CONTAINING two smaller concentric circles C_a and C_b with radii of successively a and b (see Figure B-1).

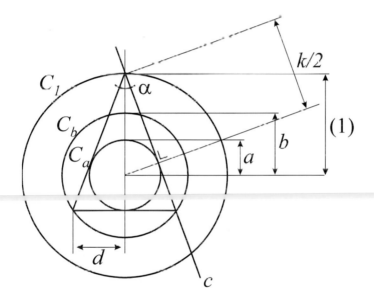

(Figure B-1

The chord c is intersected by C_1 at a length

$$k = 2\sqrt{1 - a^2} \qquad \text{[B-1]}$$

so that we can write

$$\sin\left(\frac{\alpha}{2}\right) = a,$$

[B-2]

$$\cos\left(\frac{\alpha}{2}\right) = \frac{k}{2} = \sqrt{1-a^2}$$

[B-3]

from which

$$\tan\left(\frac{\alpha}{2}\right) = \frac{a}{\sqrt{1-a^2}}.$$

[B-4]

Since $d = (1+a) \tan(\alpha/2)$ we find

$$d = a\sqrt{\frac{1+a}{1-a}}$$

[B-5]

Given that $b^2 = a^2 + d^2$, substitution of Eq. [B-5] yields

$$b = a\sqrt{\frac{2}{1-a}}.$$

[B-6]

If C_1 and C_b have to fulfill Hawkins's third theorem, we must require that

$$b = \frac{1}{2}\sqrt{2}$$

[B-7]

so that, with the aid of Eq. [B-6], we find

$$a = \frac{-1+\sqrt{17}}{8}.$$

[B-8]

From Eq. [B-2] we can now derive the top angle α of the isosceles triangle:

$$\alpha = 2\sin^{-1}\left(\frac{-1+\sqrt{17}}{8}\right)$$

[B-9]

corresponding to 45.957... degrees.

The Melick Rings

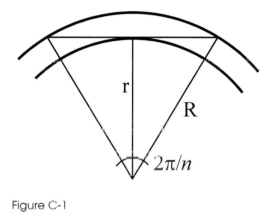

Figure C-1

WHEN TWO CONCENTRIC CIRCLES enclose an equilateral triangle, a square, a regular pentagon, a hexagon, and so forth, as shown in Figure C-1, their radii can be expressed as

$$\frac{r}{R} = \cos\left(\frac{\pi}{n}\right), \qquad\qquad \text{[C-1]}$$

Here $n = 3$ in the case of a triangle, $n = 4$ for a square, 5 for a pentagon, 6 for a hexagon, and so on. Consequently, for an equilateral triangle the ratio is $\cos(\pi/3) = 0.5$; for a square the ratio is $\cos(\pi/4) \approx 0.7071$; and for a pentagon, $\cos(\pi/5) \approx 0.8090$.

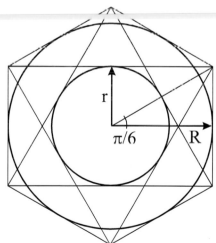

Next we consider the case of a hexagon composed of two equilateral triangles connecting two circles, as sketched in Figure C-2. In this case, from symmetry reasons, we find immediately that $r/R = \tan(\pi/6) = 1/\sqrt{3}$.

Ultimately, we consider the case of two circles connected by a pentagram and pentagon, as shown in Figure C-3.

Figure C-2

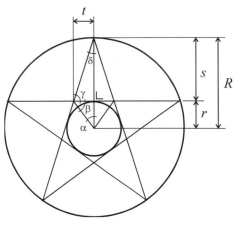

Figure C-3

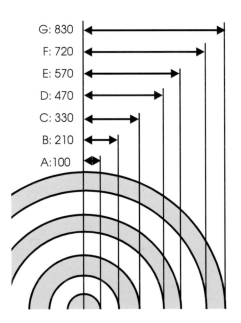

G: 830
F: 720
E: 570
D: 470
C: 330
B: 210
A:100

Figure C-4

From symmetry reasons, we find that

$$\alpha = \pi/5,$$

$$\beta = 3\pi/10,$$

$$\gamma = 2\pi/5,$$

$$\delta = \pi/10. \qquad [\text{C-2}]$$

Since

$$t = r\tan(\alpha) \qquad [\text{C-3}]$$

but also

$$t = s\tan(\delta) \qquad [\text{C-4}]$$

we find

$$\frac{r}{R} = \frac{r}{s+r} = \frac{\tan(\delta)}{\tan(\alpha)+\tan(\delta)}$$

from which

$$\frac{r}{R} = \frac{r}{s+r} = \frac{\tan(\delta)}{\tan(\alpha)+\tan(\delta)} \approx 0.3090. [\text{C-5}]$$

The radii of the rings, in centimeters, were measured as indicated in Figure C-4, with an estimated accuracy of 10 cm.

The table in Figure C-5 shows the measured values and the relative error for each radius, based on the absolute measurement in accuracy of 10 cm. Using these values, the ratios

146

between the various radii as indicated in Figures 3-10 and 3-11, as well as the absolute propagated error, is presented in the table in Figure C-6. The third column shows the exact (theoretic) values. We see that all measured values are in agreement with the theoretic values, within the margins of the measurement accuracy.

The probability that the geometric properties of the Melick rings were accidental can be approximated as follows. We define identical margins of accuracy, *d*, for each circular element, and demand that seven arbitrary radii in a range between 0 and D (defining the center circle and the inner and outer edges of the three rings) all fall within the proper margins. The chance that this will be the case amounts to

	Measured Radius (cm)	Relative Error
A	100	0.100
B	210	0.048
C	330	0.030
D	470	0.021
E	570	0.018
F	720	0.014
G	830	0.012

Figure C-5

$$\frac{7d}{D} \cdot \frac{6d}{D} \cdot \frac{5d}{D} \cdots \frac{d}{D} .$$ [C-6]

Geometric ratio by	Actual Ratio	Error	Theoretic Value
Triangle (A/B)	0.48	0.07	0.5000
Square (C/D)	0.70	0.04	0.7071
Pentagon (E/F)	0.79	0.02	0.8090
Small pentagram (A/C)	0.30	0.04	0.3090
Large Pentagram (B/F)	0.29	0.02	0.3090
Hexagram (D/G)	0.57	0.02	0.5774

Figure C-6

Taking d equal to 20 cm (based on the measuring accuracy of 10 cm), and D equal to 840 cm (the radius of the outer ring plus $d/2$), expression [C-6] results in a probability of chance of one in forty-six million. Even if we increase the margin d to the unrealistically large value of 50 centimeters, the probability of chance is still only one in seventy-five thousand. The conclusion is simple: The Melick Rings were carefully designed before the formation was created.

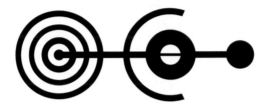

Figure C-7

Recommended Material

There is an abundance of crop circle videos and books available. An extensive list can be found on the Crop Circle Connector Web site:
www.cropcircleconnector.com/anasazi/books.html.
Here are my recommendations for further study.

Videos

Crop Circles, What on Earth Is Going On? A great, 60-minute video documentary by Bert Janssen, providing an excellent overview of the crop circle phenomenon in all its aspects, including superb footage of the mysterious balls of light. Contains interviews with prominent researchers such as Colin Andrews, Busty Taylor, ilyes, Peter Sørensen, Mark Haywood, and Michael Glickman. For more information, visit www.bertjanssen.nl.

Crop Circles, The Research. Another excellent 60-minute video by Bert Janssen, which focuses on the ideas currently being explored within the different fields of research, from biophysics to geometry. This is the best, most accurate, and most informative crop circle video I know. For more information, visit www.bertjanssen.nl.

Books

Crop Circles—A Worldwide Mystery, by Janet Ossebaard (Librero, 2000). A beautiful book, containing 275 high-quality and very artistic full-color photographs. The book discusses all aspects of the crop circle phenomenon in a most legible style, and is one of the most eye-catching and easily accessible books that has ever been written on the crop circle subject. For more information visit www.cropcircleconnector.com/Bert/janetbook2000.html.

Vital Signs, by Andy Thomas (S.B. Publications, 1998). Considered by many to be the "Crop Circle Bible." *Vital Signs* could have replaced all my other crop circle books.

The Circles Effect and Its Mysteries, by Dr. George Terence Meaden (Artetech Publishing Company, 1988). Currently out of print, but some copies may still be available somewhere. Perhaps a little dull for the general public, but excellent literature for the scientifically educated, and a must-read for the serious crop circle researcher.

Circles from the Sky, edited by Terence Meaden (Souvenir Press, 1991). Contains the proceedings of the First International Crop Circle Conference organized by Dr. Meaden in Oxford. Aimed at an audience with a technical or scientific background, and containing an abundance of very interesting findings and theories by various scientists. Another must-read for the serious crop circle researcher.

Web Sites

These sites contain many hot links to hundreds of other crop circle-related Web sites and Internet pages.

The Crop Circle Connector, www.cropcircleconnector.com.
The most prominent of all crop circle Web sites. Very big, perhaps a little cluttered, but containing lots of information and extremely up-to-date. In the summer season new formations are often reported the same morning they are discovered (including photographs and GPS coordinates!). The archive files (with information about previous years) are for members only, but the huge amounts of information, countless contributions by dozens of prominent researchers, and the astonishing photographs give members excellent value for their money.

Bert Janssen's Website, www.bertjanssen.nl/cropc/index.html.
This site contains an abundance of reliable, detailed, and in-depth information about crop circles, along with many results from original research by leading Dutch crop circle researcher Bert Janssen. In particular, the highly detailed analyses of crop circle geometry and reconstruction are very much recommended.

Crop Circle Research, www.cropcircleresearch.com.
"Dedicated to serious, scientific, and rational crop circle research." Although not all of the presented analyses can bear the scrutiny of scientific standards, the site contains much information and focuses on technical and less speculative aspects. Particularly interesting is the powerful and flexible search engine for worldwide crop circle reports.

The Crop Circular, www.lovely.clara.net/.
Overviews of all prominent British formations since 1972 by means of efficient, compact, but very complete reports. Good photographs, well designed.

Finland's Center of Circle Information, www.ioon.net/cropcircles/index.html.
A Finnish site, but written in good English. Many interesting articles and a beautiful design.

Midwest Research, www.cropcircles.org.
Website by one of America's most prominent crop circle researchers, Ron Russell. Midwest Research develops and performs special projects in the realm of New Sciences and the mysteries confronting our world.

The Circlemakers, www.circlemakers.org.
A skeptical site, created by human circlemakers. Chock-full of debunking arguments. A somewhat prejudiced and not always objective site, but containing interesting information and definitely a must-visit for the serious crop circle researcher.

Index

About the Author

Eltjo Haselhoff began his study of physics at Twente University, one of the three Dutch technical universities. After finishing the $5^1/_2$-year program in 1987, specializing in high-power gas lasers, nonlinear optics, and ultrashort optical pulse detection, he worked at several Dutch research institutes and at Los Alamos National Laboratories, USA. His main activities were in the fields of free-electron laser research, accelerator technology, ultrahigh vacuum technology, semiconductor photoemission cathodes for high-current electron beam accelerators, and ultrafast optical infrared switches. In 1993 he obtained his Ph.D. in experimental and theoretical physics after successfully defending his thesis, *Aspects of a Compton Free-Electron Laser.* Today he works in industry as senior clinical scientist in the magnetic resonance marketing department of a leading provider of medical imaging equipment.

In the strictly scientific period of his professional life (1985–1994) the author published several dozen articles in peer-reviewed scientific journals on (electro-) optics, lasers, and general matters. Since the start of his industrial career in 1995 he has been more dedicated to executive tasks. Nevertheless, he has published some scientific papers since then, one of which was related to the crop circle phenomenon.

Besides crop circles and his regular work in industry, the author has many other interests. He composes music (mainly folk, bluegrass, and jazz) and plays a handful of musical instruments (violin, acoustic and electric guitars, five-string banjo, piano, and some more). He has been a cartoonist for several regional magazines. He is a painter, a prolific photographer, designs and constructs furniture and acoustic guitars, and is skilled in woodcarving, particularly pearl inlay techniques.